CGEIT
Complete Self-Assessment

The guidance in this Self-Assessment is based on CGEIT best practices and standards in business process architecture, design and quality management. The guidance is also based on the professional judgment of the individual collaborators listed in the Acknowledgments.

Notice of rights

Table of Contents

About The Art of Service

The Art of Service, Business Process Architects since 2000, is dedicated to helping stakeholders achieve excellence.

Defining, designing, creating, and implementing a process to solve a stakeholders challenge or meet an objective is the most valuable role… In EVERY group, company, organization and department.

Unless you're talking a one-time, single-use project, there should be a process. Whether that process is managed and implemented by humans, AI, or a combination of the two, it needs to be designed by someone with a complex enough perspective to ask the right questions.

Someone capable of asking the right questions and step back and say, 'What are we really trying to accomplish here? And is there a different way to look at it?'

With The Art of Service's Standard Requirements Self-Assessments, we empower people who can do just that — whether their title is marketer, entrepreneur, manager, salesperson, consultant, Business Process Manager, executive assistant, IT Manager, CIO etc... —they are the people who rule the future. They are people who watch the process as it happens, and ask the right questions to make the process work better.

Contact us when you need any support with this Self-Assessment and any help with templates, blue-prints and examples of standard documents you might need:

http://theartofservice.com
service@theartofservice.com

Acknowledgments

This checklist was developed under the auspices of The Art of Service, chaired by Gerardus Blokdyk.

Representatives from several client companies participated in the preparation of this Self-Assessment.

In addition, we are thankful for the design and printing services provided.

Included Resources - how to access

Included with your purchase of the book is the CGEIT Self-Assessment Spreadsheet Dashboard which contains all questions and Self-Assessment areas and auto-generates insights, graphs, and project RACI planning - all with examples to get you started right away.

How? Simply send an email to
access@theartofservice.com
with this books' title in the subject to get the CGEIT Self Assessment Tool right away.

You will receive the following contents with New and Updated specific criteria:

• The latest quick edition of the book in PDF

• The latest complete edition of the book in PDF, which criteria correspond to the criteria in...

• The Self-Assessment Excel Dashboard, and...

• Example pre-filled Self-Assessment Excel Dashboard to get familiar with results generation

• In-depth specific Checklists covering the topic

• Project management checklists and templates to assist with implementation

INCLUDES LIFETIME SELF ASSESSMENT UPDATES

Every self assessment comes with Lifetime Updates and Lifetime Free Updated Books. Lifetime Updates is an industry-first feature which allows you to receive verified self assessment updates, ensuring you always have the most accurate information at your fingertips.

Get it now- you will be glad you did - do it now, before you forget.

Send an email to **access@theartofservice.com** with this books' title in the subject to get the CGEIT Self Assessment Tool right away.

Your feedback is invaluable to us

If you recently bought this book, we would love to hear from you! You can do this by writing a review on amazon (or the online store where you purchased this book) about your last purchase! As part of our continual service improvement process, we love to hear real client experiences and feedback.

How does it work?
To post a review on Amazon, just log in to your account and click on the Create Your Own Review button (under Customer Reviews) of the relevant product page. You can find examples of product reviews in Amazon. If you purchased from another online store, simply follow their procedures.

What happens when I submit my review?
Once you have submitted your review, send us an email at review@theartofservice.com with the link to your review so we can properly thank you for your feedback.

Purpose of this Self-Assessment

This Self-Assessment has been developed to improve understanding of the requirements and elements of CGEIT, based on best practices and standards in business process architecture, design and quality management.

It is designed to allow for a rapid Self-Assessment to determine how closely existing management practices and procedures correspond to the elements of the Self-Assessment.

The criteria of requirements and elements of CGEIT have been rephrased in the format of a Self-Assessment questionnaire, with a seven-criterion scoring system, as explained in this document.

In this format, even with limited background knowledge of CGEIT, a manager can quickly review existing operations to determine how they measure up to the standards. This in turn can serve as the starting point of a 'gap analysis' to identify management tools or system elements that might usefully be implemented in the organization to help improve overall performance.

How to use the Self-Assessment

On the following pages are a series of questions to identify to what extent your CGEIT initiative is complete in comparison to the requirements set in standards.

To facilitate answering the questions, there is a space in front of each question to enter a score on a scale of '1' to '5'.

1 Strongly Disagree

2 Disagree

3 Neutral

4 Agree

5 Strongly Agree

Read the question and rate it with the following in front of mind:

'In my belief,
the answer to this question is clearly defined'.

There are two ways in which you can choose to interpret this statement;

1. how aware are you that the answer to the question is clearly defined
2. for more in-depth analysis you can choose to gather evidence and confirm the answer to the question. This obviously will take more time, most Self-Assessment

users opt for the first way to interpret the question and dig deeper later on based on the outcome of the overall Self-Assessment.

A score of '1' would mean that the answer is not clear at all, where a '5' would mean the answer is crystal clear and defined. Leave emtpy when the question is not applicable or you don't want to answer it, you can skip it without affecting your score. Write your score in the space provided.

After you have responded to all the appropriate statements in each section, compute your average score for that section, using the formula provided, and round to the nearest tenth. Then transfer to the corresponding spoke in the CGEIT Scorecard on the second next page of the Self-Assessment.

Your completed CGEIT Scorecard will give you a clear presentation of which CGEIT areas need attention.

CGEIT
Scorecard Example

Example of how the finalized Scorecard can look like:

CGEIT
Scorecard

Your Scores:

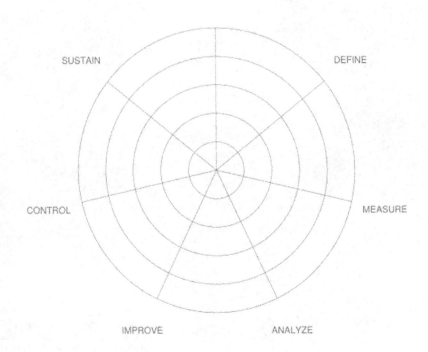

BEGINNING OF THE SELF-ASSESSMENT:

CRITERION #1: RECOGNIZE

INTENT: Be aware of the need for change. Recognize that there is an unfavorable variation, problem or symptom.

In my belief, the answer to this question is clearly defined:

5 Strongly Agree

4 Agree

3 Neutral

2 Disagree

1 Strongly Disagree

1. What vendors make products that address the CGEIT needs?
<--- Score

2. What is the smallest subset of the problem you can usefully solve?
<--- Score

3. Who had the original idea?

<--- Score

4. To what extent does each concerned units management team recognize CGEIT as an effective investment?
<--- Score

5. Will a response program recognize when a crisis occurs and provide some level of response?
<--- Score

6. What activities does the governance board need to consider?
<--- Score

7. What are your needs in relation to CGEIT skills, labor, equipment, and markets?
<--- Score

8. How well is IT positioned to meet future needs?
<--- Score

9. Are there any specific expectations or concerns about the CGEIT team, CGEIT itself?
<--- Score

10. Will new equipment/products be required to facilitate CGEIT delivery, for example is new software needed?
<--- Score

11. Is the need for organizational change recognized?
<--- Score

12. Who defines the rules in relation to any given issue?

<--- Score

13. Are there recognized CGEIT problems?
<--- Score

14. Who needs what information?
<--- Score

15. What would happen if CGEIT weren't done?
<--- Score

16. How much are sponsors, customers, partners, stakeholders involved in CGEIT? In other words, what are the risks, if CGEIT does not deliver successfully?
<--- Score

17. How can auditing be a preventative security measure?
<--- Score

18. Are you dealing with any of the same issues today as yesterday? What can you do about this?
<--- Score

19. What training and capacity building actions are needed to implement proposed reforms?
<--- Score

20. Can management personnel recognize the monetary benefit of CGEIT?
<--- Score

21. How are you going to measure success?
<--- Score

22. How are the CGEIT's objectives aligned to the

organization's overall business strategy?
<--- Score

23. Do you need to avoid or amend any CGEIT
activities?
<--- Score

24. What information do users need?
<--- Score

**25. Which techniques do you use that seeks to
identify the similarities and differences between
the groups of customers or users?**
<--- Score

26. Think about the people you identified for your
CGEIT project and the project responsibilities
you would assign to them. what kind of training
do you think they would need to perform these
responsibilities effectively?
<--- Score

27. Are controls defined to recognize and contain
problems?
<--- Score

28. What prevents you from making the changes you
know will make you a more effective CGEIT leader?
<--- Score

29. Is it clear when you think of the day ahead of you
what activities and tasks you need to complete?
<--- Score

30. Are employees recognized or rewarded for
performance that demonstrates the highest levels of

integrity?
<--- Score

31. What are the timeframes required to resolve each of the issues/problems?
<--- Score

32. Consider your own CGEIT project, what types of organizational problems do you think might be causing or affecting your problem, based on the work done so far?
<--- Score

33. To what extent would your organization benefit from being recognized as a award recipient?
<--- Score

34. What problems are you facing and how do you consider CGEIT will circumvent those obstacles?
<--- Score

35. What extra resources will you need?
<--- Score

36. What needs to be done?
<--- Score

37. Who needs to know about CGEIT?
<--- Score

38. Do you need different information or graphics?
<--- Score

39. Will CGEIT deliverables need to be tested and, if so, by whom?
<--- Score

40. How do you assess your CGEIT workforce capability and capacity needs, including skills, competencies, and staffing levels?
<--- Score

41. What are the business objectives to be achieved with CGEIT?
<--- Score

42. How do you take a forward-looking perspective in identifying CGEIT research related to market response and models?
<--- Score

43. Are your goals realistic? Do you need to redefine your problem? Perhaps the problem has changed or maybe you have reached your goal and need to set a new one?
<--- Score

44. What do you need to start doing?
<--- Score

45. When a CGEIT manager recognizes a problem, what options are available?
<--- Score

46. Looking at each person individually – does every one have the qualities which are needed to work in this group?
<--- Score

47. What are the minority interests and what amount of minority interests can be recognized?
<--- Score

48. Are problem definition and motivation clearly presented?
<--- Score

49. Do you know what you need to know about CGEIT?
<--- Score

50. What is the problem or issue?
<--- Score

51. Does CGEIT create potential expectations in other areas that need to be recognized and considered?
<--- Score

52. What tools and technologies are needed for a custom CGEIT project?
<--- Score

53. Should you invest in industry-recognized qualications?
<--- Score

54. Who else hopes to benefit from it?
<--- Score

55. What else needs to be measured?
<--- Score

56. What should be considered when identifying available resources, constraints, and deadlines?
<--- Score

57. How do you identify the kinds of information that you will need?

<--- Score

58. Are there CGEIT problems defined?
<--- Score

59. Will it solve real problems?
<--- Score

60. Do you have/need 24-hour access to key personnel?
<--- Score

61. For your CGEIT project, identify and describe the business environment, is there more than one layer to the business environment?
<--- Score

62. Are there any revenue recognition issues?
<--- Score

63. What does CGEIT success mean to the stakeholders?
<--- Score

64. Who are your key stakeholders who need to sign off?
<--- Score

65. As a sponsor, customer or management, how important is it to meet goals, objectives?
<--- Score

66. Have you identified your CGEIT key performance indicators?
<--- Score

67. What situation(s) led to this CGEIT Self Assessment?
<--- Score

68. How does it fit into your organizational needs and tasks?
<--- Score

69. What are the expected benefits of CGEIT to the business?
<--- Score

70. Does your organization need more CGEIT education?
<--- Score

Add up total points for this section:
_ _ _ _ _ = Total points for this section

Divided by: _ _ _ _ _ _ (number of statements answered) = _ _ _ _ _ _
Average score for this section

Transfer your score to the CGEIT Index at the beginning of the Self-Assessment.

CRITERION #2: DEFINE:

INTENT: Formulate the business problem. Define the problem, needs and objectives.

In my belief, the answer to this question is clearly defined:

5 Strongly Agree

4 Agree

3 Neutral

2 Disagree

1 Strongly Disagree

1. What would be the goal or target for a CGEIT's improvement team?
<--- Score

2. In what way can you redefine the criteria of choice clients have in your category in your favor?
<--- Score

3. Has a high-level 'as is' process map been completed,

verified and validated?
<--- Score

4. Has/have the customer(s) been identified?
<--- Score

5. How would you define the culture at your organization, how susceptible is it to CGEIT changes?
<--- Score

6. Is the CGEIT scope manageable?
<--- Score

7. Are roles and responsibilities formally defined?
<--- Score

8. Is the scope of CGEIT defined?
<--- Score

9. Do you all define CGEIT in the same way?
<--- Score

10. Have specific policy objectives been defined?
<--- Score

11. What scope to assess?
<--- Score

12. Which elements are still required to implement a good IT governance framework?
<--- Score

13. Is there regularly 100% attendance at the team meetings? If not, have appointed substitutes attended to preserve cross-functionality and full representation?

<--- Score

14. What customer feedback methods were used to solicit their input?
<--- Score

15. What sources do you use to gather information for a CGEIT study?
<--- Score

16. Is a fully trained team formed, supported, and committed to work on the CGEIT improvements?
<--- Score

17. Is full participation by members in regularly held team meetings guaranteed?
<--- Score

18. How do you hand over CGEIT context?
<--- Score

19. When are meeting minutes sent out? Who is on the distribution list?
<--- Score

20. When was the CGEIT start date?
<--- Score

21. Are there different segments of customers?
<--- Score

22. What are the Roles and Responsibilities for each team member and its leadership? Where is this documented?
<--- Score

23. Have the customer needs been translated into specific, measurable requirements? How?
<--- Score

24. Is there a CGEIT management charter, including business case, problem and goal statements, scope, milestones, roles and responsibilities, communication plan?
<--- Score

25. Is there a completed SIPOC representation, describing the Suppliers, Inputs, Process, Outputs, and Customers?
<--- Score

26. Are business processes mapped?
<--- Score

27. Has the CGEIT work been fairly and/or equitably divided and delegated among team members who are qualified and capable to perform the work? Has everyone contributed?
<--- Score

28. Has the direction changed at all during the course of CGEIT? If so, when did it change and why?
<--- Score

29. What defines best in class?
<--- Score

30. Are required metrics defined, what are they?
<--- Score

31. How was the 'as is' process map developed, reviewed, verified and validated?

<--- Score

32. Are customer(s) identified and segmented according to their different needs and requirements?
<--- Score

33. What are the boundaries of the scope? What is in bounds and what is not? What is the start point? What is the stop point?
<--- Score

34. How do you keep key subject matter experts in the loop?
<--- Score

35. Why are you doing CGEIT and what is the scope?
<--- Score

36. Is the team sponsored by a champion or business leader?
<--- Score

37. What system do you use for gathering CGEIT information?
<--- Score

38. Is it clearly defined in and to your organization what you do?
<--- Score

39. Is the team formed and are team leaders (Coaches and Management Leads) assigned?
<--- Score

40. Has a project plan, Gantt chart, or similar been developed/completed?

<--- Score

41. What is the context?
<--- Score

42. Are improvement team members fully trained on CGEIT?
<--- Score

43. When is the estimated completion date?
<--- Score

44. Have all of the relationships been defined properly?
<--- Score

45. How will variation in the actual durations of each activity be dealt with to ensure that the expected CGEIT results are met?
<--- Score

46. Is there a completed, verified, and validated high-level 'as is' (not 'should be' or 'could be') business process map?
<--- Score

47. How can the value of CGEIT be defined?
<--- Score

48. Has anyone else (internal or external to the organization) attempted to solve this problem or a similar one before? If so, what knowledge can be leveraged from these previous efforts?
<--- Score

49. How is the team tracking and documenting its

work?
<--- Score

50. Is CGEIT currently on schedule according to the plan?
<--- Score

51. Is the team equipped with available and reliable resources?
<--- Score

52. Do the problem and goal statements meet the SMART criteria (specific, measurable, attainable, relevant, and time-bound)?
<--- Score

53. Will team members perform CGEIT work when assigned and in a timely fashion?
<--- Score

54. What key business process output measure(s) does CGEIT leverage and how?
<--- Score

55. How and when will the baselines be defined?
<--- Score

56. Does the team have regular meetings?
<--- Score

57. Are customers identified and high impact areas defined?
<--- Score

58. Is the team adequately staffed with the desired cross-functionality? If not, what additional resources

are available to the team?
<--- Score

59. Is scope creep really all bad news?
<--- Score

60. What are the rough order estimates on cost savings/opportunities that CGEIT brings?
<--- Score

61. What is out-of-scope initially?
<--- Score

62. What is the scope of the CGEIT effort?
<--- Score

63. Will team members regularly document their CGEIT work?
<--- Score

64. Has the improvement team collected the 'voice of the customer' (obtained feedback – qualitative and quantitative)?
<--- Score

65. What are the dynamics of the communication plan?
<--- Score

66. What critical content must be communicated – who, what, when, where, and how?
<--- Score

67. Is there a critical path to deliver CGEIT results?
<--- Score

68. Does the scope remain the same?
<--- Score

69. What happens if CGEIT's scope changes?
<--- Score

70. What scope do you want your strategy to cover?
<--- Score

71. Is CGEIT linked to key business goals and objectives?
<--- Score

72. What are the record-keeping requirements of CGEIT activities?
<--- Score

73. What are the tasks and definitions?
<--- Score

74. Are accountability and ownership for CGEIT clearly defined?
<--- Score

75. What specifically is the problem? Where does it occur? When does it occur? What is its extent?
<--- Score

76. How did the CGEIT manager receive input to the development of a CGEIT improvement plan and the estimated completion dates/times of each activity?
<--- Score

77. What baselines are required to be defined and managed?
<--- Score

78. What is the definition of success?
<--- Score

79. Who defines (or who defined) the rules and roles?
<--- Score

80. If substitutes have been appointed, have they
been briefed on the CGEIT goals and received regular
communications as to the progress to date?
<--- Score

81. What is the scope of CGEIT?
<--- Score

82. Is the improvement team aware of the different
versions of a process: what they think it is vs. what it
actually is vs. what it should be vs. what it could be?
<--- Score

83. What is out of scope?
<--- Score

84. What was the context?
<--- Score

85. What is in the scope and what is not in scope?
<--- Score

86. Are there any constraints known that bear on
the ability to perform CGEIT work? How is the team
addressing them?
<--- Score

87. Is CGEIT required?
<--- Score

88. How does the CGEIT manager ensure against scope creep?
<--- Score

89. Scope of sensitive information?
<--- Score

90. Are task requirements clearly defined?
<--- Score

91. How do you gather CGEIT requirements?
<--- Score

92. Are approval levels defined for contracts and supplements to contracts?
<--- Score

93. How often are the team meetings?
<--- Score

94. How would you define CGEIT leadership?
<--- Score

95. What is in scope?
<--- Score

96. Who are the CGEIT improvement team members, including Management Leads and Coaches?
<--- Score

97. Has your scope been defined?
<--- Score

98. Are different versions of process maps needed to account for the different types of inputs?

<--- Score

99. Are team charters developed?
<--- Score

100. How will the CGEIT team and the organization measure complete success of CGEIT?
<--- Score

101. How do you think the partners involved in CGEIT would have defined success?
<--- Score

102. Have all basic functions of CGEIT been defined?
<--- Score

103. What are the compelling business reasons for embarking on CGEIT?
<--- Score

104. Is the current 'as is' process being followed? If not, what are the discrepancies?
<--- Score

105. Are resources adequate for the scope?
<--- Score

106. What constraints exist that might impact the team?
<--- Score

107. Is data collected and displayed to better understand customer(s) critical needs and requirements.
<--- Score

108. Is the CGEIT scope complete and appropriately sized?
<--- Score

109. What CGEIT requirements should be gathered?
<--- Score

110. Who is gathering CGEIT information?
<--- Score

111. How do you manage scope?
<--- Score

112. Are audit criteria, scope, frequency and methods defined?
<--- Score

113. Has everyone on the team, including the team leaders, been properly trained?
<--- Score

114. Has a team charter been developed and communicated?
<--- Score

Add up total points for this section:
_ _ _ _ _ = Total points for this section

Divided by: _ _ _ _ _ _ (number of statements answered) = _ _ _ _ _ _
Average score for this section

Transfer your score to the CGEIT Index at the beginning of the Self-Assessment.

CRITERION #3: MEASURE:

INTENT: Gather the correct data.
Measure the current performance and
evolution of the situation.

In my belief, the answer to this
question is clearly defined:

5 Strongly Agree

4 Agree

3 Neutral

2 Disagree

1 Strongly Disagree

1. Are the units of measure consistent?
<--- Score

2. Is data collection planned and executed?
<--- Score

3. The approach of traditional CGEIT works for detail complexity but is focused on a systematic approach rather than an understanding of the nature of

systems themselves, what approach will permit your organization to deal with the kind of unpredictable emergent behaviors that dynamic complexity can introduce?
<--- Score

4. Have all non-recommended alternatives been analyzed in sufficient detail?
<--- Score

5. Which measures and indicators matter?
<--- Score

6. How do you measure success?
<--- Score

7. How do you control the overall costs of your work processes?
<--- Score

8. Does your organization systematically track and analyze outcomes related for accountability and quality improvement?
<--- Score

9. Are you aware of what could cause a problem?
<--- Score

10. How will measures be used to manage and adapt?
<--- Score

11. How do you focus on what is right -not who is right?
<--- Score

12. From balanced scorecard to strategic gauges:

is measurement worth it?
<--- Score

13. What are the costs of reform?
<--- Score

14. What causes mismanagement?
<--- Score

15. Who should receive measurement reports?
<--- Score

16. Among the CGEIT product and service cost to be estimated, which is considered hardest to estimate?
<--- Score

17. How will success or failure be measured?
<--- Score

18. What measurements are possible, practicable and meaningful?
<--- Score

19. Are process variation components displayed/ communicated using suitable charts, graphs, plots?
<--- Score

20. Is long term and short term variability accounted for?
<--- Score

21. How do you aggregate measures across priorities?
<--- Score

22. What measurements are being captured?
<--- Score

23. Does CGEIT analysis isolate the fundamental causes of problems?
<--- Score

24. What causes investor action?
<--- Score

25. How is progress measured?
<--- Score

26. Why do the measurements/indicators matter?
<--- Score

27. Which roles are responsible for review and risk analysis of all contracts on a regular basis?
<--- Score

28. How do you identify and analyze stakeholders and their interests?
<--- Score

29. What could cause delays in the schedule?
<--- Score

30. What causes innovation to fail or succeed in your organization?
<--- Score

31. Can you do CGEIT without complex (expensive) analysis?
<--- Score

32. What is measured? Why?
<--- Score

33. How frequently do you track CGEIT measures?
<--- Score

34. Can you measure the return on analysis?
<--- Score

35. How to cause the change?
<--- Score

36. How will effects be measured?
<--- Score

37. How will you measure your CGEIT effectiveness?
<--- Score

38. Is it possible to estimate the impact of unanticipated complexity such as wrong or failed assumptions, feedback, etc. on proposed reforms?
<--- Score

39. How do you stay flexible and focused to recognize larger CGEIT results?
<--- Score

40. What are the types and number of measures to use?
<--- Score

41. Are there measurements based on task performance?
<--- Score

42. Is there a Performance Baseline?
<--- Score

43. Have the types of risks that may impact CGEIT

been identified and analyzed?
<--- Score

44. What could cause you to change course?
<--- Score

45. What causes extra work or rework?
<--- Score

46. How do you do risk analysis of rare, cascading, catastrophic events?
<--- Score

47. Did you tackle the cause or the symptom?
<--- Score

48. What are the key input variables? What are the key process variables? What are the key output variables?
<--- Score

49. What particular quality tools did the team find helpful in establishing measurements?
<--- Score

50. Which factors will you not consider for the SWOT analysis?
<--- Score

51. How is performance measured?
<--- Score

52. Do supply chain IT alignment and supply chain interfirm system integration impact upon brand equity and organization performance?
<--- Score

53. What do you measure and why?
<--- Score

54. Have you found any 'ground fruit' or 'low-hanging fruit' for immediate remedies to the gap in performance?
<--- Score

55. Will CGEIT have an impact on current business continuity, disaster recovery processes and/or infrastructure?
<--- Score

56. Was a data collection plan established?
<--- Score

57. How will you measure success?
<--- Score

58. Is key measure data collection planned and executed, process variation displayed and communicated and performance baselined?
<--- Score

59. How are measurements made?
<--- Score

60. How is the value delivered by CGEIT being measured?
<--- Score

61. Is the solution cost-effective?
<--- Score

62. Are missed CGEIT opportunities costing your organization money?

<--- Score

63. Do you effectively measure and reward individual and team performance?
<--- Score

64. What key measures identified indicate the performance of the business process?
<--- Score

65. Does CGEIT analysis show the relationships among important CGEIT factors?
<--- Score

66. Which stakeholder characteristics are analyzed?
<--- Score

67. Does the CGEIT task fit the client's priorities?
<--- Score

68. Is Process Variation Displayed/Communicated?
<--- Score

69. Are key measures identified and agreed upon?
<--- Score

70. Are high impact defects defined and identified in the business process?
<--- Score

71. What are your key CGEIT indicators that you will measure, analyze and track?
<--- Score

72. How do you measure efficient delivery of CGEIT services?

<--- Score

73. How do you measure lifecycle phases?
<--- Score

74. Is a solid data collection plan established that includes measurement systems analysis?
<--- Score

75. How can you measure the performance?
<--- Score

76. Are losses documented, analyzed, and remedial processes developed to prevent future losses?
<--- Score

77. What harm might be caused?
<--- Score

78. What are the uncertainties surrounding estimates of impact?
<--- Score

79. What methods are feasible and acceptable to estimate the impact of reforms?
<--- Score

80. Have changes been properly/adequately analyzed for effect?
<--- Score

81. Does CGEIT systematically track and analyze outcomes for accountability and quality improvement?
<--- Score

82. What relevant entities could be measured?
<--- Score

83. Have you made assumptions about the shape of the future, particularly its impact on your customers and competitors?
<--- Score

84. Do staff have the necessary skills to collect, analyze, and report data?
<--- Score

85. Why do you expend time and effort to implement measurement, for whom?
<--- Score

86. What does it cost?
<--- Score

87. What would be a real cause for concern?
<--- Score

88. What has the team done to assure the stability and accuracy of the measurement process?
<--- Score

89. What is an unallowable cost?
<--- Score

90. Are the measurements objective?
<--- Score

91. What is the right balance of time and resources between investigation, analysis, and discussion and dissemination?
<--- Score

92. Who participated in the data collection for measurements?
<--- Score

93. How will your organization measure success?
<--- Score

94. How do you control the cost of IT?
<--- Score

95. Is data collected on key measures that were identified?
<--- Score

96. How can you measure CGEIT in a systematic way?
<--- Score

97. What evidence is there and what is measured?
<--- Score

98. What charts has the team used to display the components of variation in the process?
<--- Score

99. Have the concerns of stakeholders to help identify and define potential barriers been obtained and analyzed?
<--- Score

100. What are your key CGEIT organizational performance measures, including key short and longer-term financial measures?
<--- Score

101. What are the agreed upon definitions of the high

impact areas, defect(s), unit(s), and opportunities that will figure into the process capability metrics?
<--- Score

102. Are there any easy-to-implement alternatives to CGEIT? Sometimes other solutions are available that do not require the cost implications of a full-blown project?
<--- Score

103. How do you know that any CGEIT analysis is complete and comprehensive?
<--- Score

104. Where is it measured?
<--- Score

105. How large is the gap between current performance and the customer-specified (goal) performance?
<--- Score

106. What data was collected (past, present, future/ongoing)?
<--- Score

107. What are your customers expectations and measures?
<--- Score

108. What potential environmental factors impact the CGEIT effort?
<--- Score

109. What disadvantage does this cause for the user?
<--- Score

110. How do you measure variability?
<--- Score

111. How will we measure whether the communications strategy achieves its objectives?
<--- Score

112. Are you taking your company in the direction of better and revenue or cheaper and cost?
<--- Score

113. How do your measurements capture actionable CGEIT information for use in exceeding your customers expectations and securing your customers engagement?
<--- Score

114. Do you aggressively reward and promote the people who have the biggest impact on creating excellent CGEIT services/products?
<--- Score

Add up total points for this section:
_ _ _ _ _ = Total points for this section

Divided by: _ _ _ _ _ _ (number of statements answered) = _ _ _ _ _ _
Average score for this section

Transfer your score to the CGEIT Index at the beginning of the Self-Assessment.

CRITERION #4: ANALYZE:

INTENT: Analyze causes, assumptions and hypotheses.

In my belief, the answer to this question is clearly defined:

5 Strongly Agree

4 Agree

3 Neutral

2 Disagree

1 Strongly Disagree

1. How does the organization define, manage, and improve its CGEIT processes?
<--- Score

2. How do you measure the operational performance of your key work systems and processes, including productivity, cycle time, and other appropriate measures of process effectiveness, efficiency, and innovation?
<--- Score

3. Were any designed experiments used to generate additional insight into the data analysis?
<--- Score

4. How effective and efficient are the IT processes?
<--- Score

5. What processes and assets need protection?
<--- Score

6. Do your leaders quickly bounce back from setbacks?
<--- Score

7. How often will data be collected for measures?
<--- Score

8. Record-keeping requirements flow from the records needed as inputs, outputs, controls and for transformation of a CGEIT process. Are the records needed as inputs to the CGEIT process available?
<--- Score

9. Do your contracts/agreements contain data security obligations?
<--- Score

10. Is the performance gap determined?
<--- Score

11. An organizationally feasible system request is one that considers the mission, goals and objectives of the organization. Key questions are: is the CGEIT solution request practical and will it solve a problem or take advantage of an opportunity to achieve company

goals?

<--- Score

12. Have the problem and goal statements been updated to reflect the additional knowledge gained from the analyze phase?

<--- Score

13. Do your employees have the opportunity to do what they do best everyday?

<--- Score

14. Is the required CGEIT data gathered?

<--- Score

15. Is Data and process analysis, root cause analysis and quantifying the gap/opportunity in place?

<--- Score

16. When conducting a business process reengineering study, what do you look for when trying to identify business processes to change?

<--- Score

17. Were there any improvement opportunities identified from the process analysis?

<--- Score

18. Did any additional data need to be collected?

<--- Score

19. Which types of benefits are provided by a new IT-driven initiative for IT investment program?

<--- Score

20. How do you use CGEIT data and information

to support organizational decision making and innovation?
<--- Score

21. What are your best practices for minimizing CGEIT project risk, while demonstrating incremental value and quick wins throughout the CGEIT project lifecycle?
<--- Score

22. Have any additional benefits been identified that will result from closing all or most of the gaps?
<--- Score

23. What CGEIT data do you gather or use now?
<--- Score

24. Do you, as a leader, bounce back quickly from setbacks?
<--- Score

25. How do you implement and manage your work processes to ensure that they meet design requirements?
<--- Score

26. Were Pareto charts (or similar) used to portray the 'heavy hitters' (or key sources of variation)?
<--- Score

27. What controls do you have in place to protect data?
<--- Score

28. What are the disruptive CGEIT technologies that enable your organization to radically change your

business processes?
<--- Score

29. Can you add value to the current CGEIT decision-making process (largely qualitative) by incorporating uncertainty modeling (more quantitative)?
<--- Score

30. Is the suppliers process defined and controlled?
<--- Score

31. Did any value-added analysis or 'lean thinking' take place to identify some of the gaps shown on the 'as is' process map?
<--- Score

32. What other jobs or tasks affect the performance of the steps in the CGEIT process?
<--- Score

33. What are your key performance measures or indicators and in-process measures for the control and improvement of your CGEIT processes?
<--- Score

34. What critical business processes are dependent on IT, and what are the requirements of business processes?
<--- Score

35. Do several people in different organizational units assist with the CGEIT process?
<--- Score

36. How do your work systems and key work processes relate to and capitalize on your core

competencies?
<--- Score

37. What other organizational variables, such as reward systems or communication systems, affect the performance of this CGEIT process?
<--- Score

38. What were the crucial 'moments of truth' on the process map?
<--- Score

39. What is the cost of poor quality as supported by the team's analysis?
<--- Score

40. Which steps are performed in the IT strategy formulation process?
<--- Score

41. How is CGEIT data gathered?
<--- Score

42. Identify an operational issue in your organization. for example, could a particular task be done more quickly or more efficiently by CGEIT?
<--- Score

43. What process should you select for improvement?
<--- Score

44. Are CGEIT changes recognized early enough to be approved through the regular process?
<--- Score

45. Where is CGEIT data gathered?

<--- Score

46. What did the team gain from developing a sub-process map?
<--- Score

47. How do you identify specific CGEIT investment opportunities and emerging trends?
<--- Score

48. What methods do you use to gather CGEIT data?
<--- Score

49. What is the major goal of risk management in the decision-making process?
<--- Score

50. Is Your organization Ready for a Big Data Breach?
<--- Score

51. What does the data say about the performance of the business process?
<--- Score

52. Is the gap/opportunity displayed and communicated in financial terms?
<--- Score

53. What tools were used to narrow the list of possible causes?
<--- Score

54. What are your CGEIT processes?
<--- Score

55. Was a detailed process map created to amplify critical steps of the 'as is' business process?
<--- Score

56. Think about some of the processes you undertake within your organization, which do you own?
<--- Score

57. How do you promote understanding that opportunity for improvement is not criticism of the status quo, or the people who created the status quo?
<--- Score

58. How quickly can you capture the records of key players (what IT resources do you need)?
<--- Score

59. Where is the data coming from to measure compliance?
<--- Score

60. Internal Knowledge management capabilities: how does your organization support its internal business process?
<--- Score

61. How was the detailed process map generated, verified, and validated?
<--- Score

62. Think about the functions involved in your CGEIT project, what processes flow from these functions?
<--- Score

63. What successful thing are you doing today that may be blinding you to new growth opportunities?

<--- Score

64. A compounding model resolution with available relevant data can often provide insight towards a solution methodology; which CGEIT models, tools and techniques are necessary?
<--- Score

65. What conclusions were drawn from the team's data collection and analysis? How did the team reach these conclusions?
<--- Score

66. What data is gathered?
<--- Score

67. Is the CGEIT process severely broken such that a re-design is necessary?
<--- Score

68. How is the way you as the leader think and process information affecting your organizational culture?
<--- Score

69. What tools were used to generate the list of possible causes?
<--- Score

70. What were the financial benefits resulting from any 'ground fruit or low-hanging fruit' (quick fixes)?
<--- Score

71. What are your current levels and trends in key CGEIT measures or indicators of product and process performance that are important to and directly serve your customers?

<--- Score

72. Was a cause-and-effect diagram used to explore the different types of causes (or sources of variation)?
<--- Score

73. What will drive CGEIT change?
<--- Score

74. What are the best opportunities for value improvement?
<--- Score

75. What are the revised rough estimates of the financial savings/opportunity for CGEIT improvements?
<--- Score

76. How do mission and objectives affect the CGEIT processes of your organization?
<--- Score

77. What are your current levels and trends in key measures or indicators of CGEIT product and process performance that are important to and directly serve your customers? How do these results compare with the performance of your competitors and other organizations with similar offerings?
<--- Score

78. What is your organizations process which leads to recognition of value generation?
<--- Score

79. How are metrics used to drive transparency in selecting and implementing both tactical and

strategic improvement projects?
<--- Score

80. What quality tools were used to get through the analyze phase?
<--- Score

81. Are gaps between current performance and the goal performance identified?
<--- Score

Add up total points for this section:
_____ = Total points for this section

Divided by: _____ (number of statements answered) = _____
Average score for this section

Transfer your score to the CGEIT Index at the beginning of the Self-Assessment.

CRITERION #5: IMPROVE:

INTENT: Develop a practical solution.
Innovate, establish and test the
solution and to measure the results.

In my belief, the answer to this
question is clearly defined:

5 Strongly Agree

4 Agree

3 Neutral

2 Disagree

1 Strongly Disagree

1. How do you measure progress and evaluate
training effectiveness?
<--- Score

2. What is the risk?
<--- Score

3. How do you link measurement and risk?
<--- Score

4. What type of risk response is being audited?
<--- Score

5. How did the team generate the list of possible solutions?
<--- Score

6. How do you improve your likelihood of success ?
<--- Score

7. Are possible solutions generated and tested?
<--- Score

8. Is the scope clearly documented?
<--- Score

9. What went well, what should change, what can improve?
<--- Score

10. Can you identify any significant risks or exposures to CGEIT third- parties (vendors, service providers, alliance partners etc) that concern you?
<--- Score

11. Is the implementation plan designed?
<--- Score

12. What current systems have to be understood and/ or changed?
<--- Score

13. Which types of project tends to have more well-understood risks?
<--- Score

14. What tools were used to evaluate the potential solutions?
<--- Score

15. How do you decide how much to remunerate an employee?
<--- Score

16. Are you assessing CGEIT and risk?
<--- Score

17. How do you measure risk?
<--- Score

18. Explorations of the frontiers of CGEIT will help you build influence, improve CGEIT, optimize decision making, and sustain change, what is your approach?
<--- Score

19. How can you improve performance?
<--- Score

20. What does the 'should be' process map/design look like?
<--- Score

21. Are improved process ('should be') maps modified based on pilot data and analysis?
<--- Score

22. Can the solution be designed and implemented within an acceptable time period?
<--- Score

23. For estimation problems, how do you develop an

estimation statement?

<--- Score

24. What improvements have been achieved?

<--- Score

25. Are stakeholders aware of the Framework for Improving Critical Infrastructure Cybersecurity ?

<--- Score

26. How risky is your organization?

<--- Score

27. Risk factors: what are the characteristics of CGEIT that make it risky?

<--- Score

28. How will the team or the process owner(s) monitor the implementation plan to see that it is working as intended?

<--- Score

29. How do you improve productivity?

<--- Score

30. What error proofing will be done to address some of the discrepancies observed in the 'as is' process?

<--- Score

31. Are new and improved process ('should be') maps developed?

<--- Score

32. How will you know when its improved?

<--- Score

33. Was a pilot designed for the proposed solution(s)?
<--- Score

34. Is the solution technically practical?
<--- Score

35. What communications are necessary to support the implementation of the solution?
<--- Score

36. How will you know that you have improved?
<--- Score

37. How will the organization know that the solution worked?
<--- Score

38. Do those selected for the CGEIT team have a good general understanding of what CGEIT is all about?
<--- Score

39. How does the team improve its work?
<--- Score

40. To what extent does management recognize CGEIT as a tool to increase the results?
<--- Score

41. Risk Identification: What are the possible risk events your organization faces in relation to CGEIT?
<--- Score

42. Where will you define the frequency of risk audits?
<--- Score

43. What should a proof of concept or pilot accomplish?
<--- Score

44. What were the underlying assumptions on the cost-benefit analysis?
<--- Score

45. What is the CGEIT's sustainability risk?
<--- Score

46. At what point will vulnerability assessments be performed once CGEIT is put into production (e.g., ongoing Risk Management after implementation)?
<--- Score

47. How do you go about comparing CGEIT approaches/solutions?
<--- Score

48. Who are the people involved in developing and implementing CGEIT?
<--- Score

49. What to do with the results or outcomes of measurements?
<--- Score

50. Why improve in the first place?
<--- Score

51. How do the CGEIT results compare with the performance of your competitors and other organizations with similar offerings?
<--- Score

52. Have you identified breakpoints and/or risk tolerances that will trigger broad consideration of a potential need for intervention or modification of strategy?
<--- Score

53. Is there a high likelihood that any recommendations will achieve their intended results?
<--- Score

54. Do you cover the five essential competencies: Communication, Collaboration,Innovation, Adaptability, and Leadership that improve an organization's ability to leverage the new CGEIT in a volatile global economy?
<--- Score

55. In the past few months, what is the smallest change you have made that has had the biggest positive result? What was it about that small change that produced the large return?
<--- Score

56. What resources are required for the improvement efforts?
<--- Score

57. Which of the recognised risks out of all risks can be most likely transferred?
<--- Score

58. What is the implementation plan?
<--- Score

59. How do you create a shared risk assessment framework?

<--- Score

60. What actually has to improve and by how much?
<--- Score

61. How can you improve CGEIT?
<--- Score

62. Which techniques are used for understanding the environment in which the business operates?
<--- Score

63. Is a contingency plan established?
<--- Score

64. What tools were most useful during the improve phase?
<--- Score

65. What should the project manager do with a risk event?
<--- Score

66. Who will be using the results of the measurement activities?
<--- Score

67. Which risks refer to the risks associated with an event in the absence of specific controls?
<--- Score

68. Is there a small-scale pilot for proposed improvement(s)? What conclusions were drawn from the outcomes of a pilot?
<--- Score

69. Who will be responsible for making the decisions to include or exclude requested changes once CGEIT is underway?
<--- Score

70. Who will be responsible for documenting the CGEIT requirements in detail?
<--- Score

71. Is the optimal solution selected based on testing and analysis?
<--- Score

72. Who controls the risk?
<--- Score

73. Does the goal represent a desired result that can be measured?
<--- Score

74. Is the measure of success for CGEIT understandable to a variety of people?
<--- Score

75. How can skill-level changes improve CGEIT?
<--- Score

76. What tools do you use once you have decided on a CGEIT strategy and more importantly how do you choose?
<--- Score

77. Who controls key decisions that will be made?
<--- Score

78. What is CGEIT's impact on utilizing the best

solution(s)?
<--- Score

79. Will the controls trigger any other risks?
<--- Score

80. Were any criteria developed to assist the team in testing and evaluating potential solutions?
<--- Score

81. What can you do to improve?
<--- Score

82. What are your current levels and trends in key measures or indicators of workforce and leader development?
<--- Score

83. Is there a cost/benefit analysis of optimal solution(s)?
<--- Score

84. How long does it take to make major IT decisions?
<--- Score

85. Describe the design of the pilot and what tests were conducted, if any?
<--- Score

86. How do you improve CGEIT service perception, and satisfaction?
<--- Score

87. How significant is the improvement in the eyes of the end user?

<--- Score

88. Is a solution implementation plan established, including schedule/work breakdown structure, resources, risk management plan, cost/budget, and control plan?
<--- Score

89. Risk events: what are the things that could go wrong?
<--- Score

90. Which strategies will you use to tackle the risks?
<--- Score

91. Is pilot data collected and analyzed?
<--- Score

92. Are risk triggers captured?
<--- Score

93. What practices helps your organization to develop its capacity to recognize patterns?
<--- Score

94. What is the team's contingency plan for potential problems occurring in implementation?
<--- Score

95. Is supporting CGEIT documentation required?
<--- Score

96. What do you want to improve?
<--- Score

97. What attendant changes will need to be made to ensure that the solution is successful?
<--- Score

98. What lessons, if any, from a pilot were incorporated into the design of the full-scale solution?
<--- Score

99. Are the best solutions selected?
<--- Score

100. For decision problems, how do you develop a decision statement?
<--- Score

101. How do you define the solutions' scope?
<--- Score

102. How do you improve business agility through a more flexible IT environment?
<--- Score

103. How does the solution remove the key sources of issues discovered in the analyze phase?
<--- Score

104. How do you keep improving CGEIT?
<--- Score

105. Are there any constraints (technical, political, cultural, or otherwise) that would inhibit certain solutions?
<--- Score

106. How will you know that a change is an improvement?

<--- Score

107. What is the magnitude of the improvements?
<--- Score

108. What tools were used to tap into the creativity
and encourage 'outside the box' thinking?
<--- Score

109. How do you manage and improve your CGEIT
work systems to deliver customer value and achieve
organizational success and sustainability?
<--- Score

110. Do you combine technical expertise with
business knowledge and CGEIT Key topics include
lifecycles, development approaches, requirements
and how to make a business case?
<--- Score

111. How will you measure the results?
<--- Score

112. If you could go back in time five years, what
decision would you make differently? What is your
best guess as to what decision you're making today
you might regret five years from now?
<--- Score

113. What needs improvement? Why?
<--- Score

114. How do you measure improved CGEIT service
perception, and satisfaction?
<--- Score

115. What are the implications of the one critical CGEIT decision 10 minutes, 10 months, and 10 years from now?
<--- Score

Add up total points for this section:
_____ = Total points for this section

Divided by: _____ (number of statements answered) = _____
Average score for this section

Transfer your score to the CGEIT Index at the beginning of the Self-Assessment.

CRITERION #6: CONTROL:

INTENT: Implement the practical solution. Maintain the performance and correct possible complications.

In my belief, the answer to this question is clearly defined:

5 Strongly Agree

4 Agree

3 Neutral

2 Disagree

1 Strongly Disagree

1. Where do ideas that reach policy makers and planners as proposals for CGEIT strengthening and reform actually originate?
<--- Score

2. How is change control managed?
<--- Score

3. What is the best design framework for CGEIT

organization now that, in a post industrial-age if the top-down, command and control model is no longer relevant?

<--- Score

4. What are the known security controls?

<--- Score

5. Will existing staff require re-training, for example, to learn new business processes?

<--- Score

6. What are you attempting to measure/monitor?

<--- Score

7. Have new or revised work instructions resulted?

<--- Score

8. Is there documentation that will support the successful operation of the improvement?

<--- Score

9. Is knowledge gained on process shared and institutionalized?

<--- Score

10. What other systems, operations, processes, and infrastructures (hiring practices, staffing, training, incentives/rewards, metrics/dashboards/scorecards, etc.) need updates, additions, changes, or deletions in order to facilitate knowledge transfer and improvements?

<--- Score

11. Does the response plan contain a definite closed loop continual improvement scheme (e.g., plan-do-

check-act)?

<--- Score

12. What can you control?

<--- Score

13. How do your controls stack up?

<--- Score

14. Are pertinent alerts monitored, analyzed and distributed to appropriate personnel?

<--- Score

15. Who is the CGEIT process owner?

<--- Score

16. Is there a documented and implemented monitoring plan?

<--- Score

17. Is a response plan in place for when the input, process, or output measures indicate an 'out-of-control' condition?

<--- Score

18. Is there a transfer of ownership and knowledge to process owner and process team tasked with the responsibilities.

<--- Score

19. What are the key elements of your CGEIT performance improvement system, including your evaluation, organizational learning, and innovation processes?

<--- Score

20. What is the control/monitoring plan?
<--- Score

21. How will the day-to-day responsibilities for monitoring and continual improvement be transferred from the improvement team to the process owner?
<--- Score

22. What should you measure to verify efficiency gains?
<--- Score

23. Is reporting being used or needed?
<--- Score

24. How do you encourage people to take control and responsibility?
<--- Score

25. Does a troubleshooting guide exist or is it needed?
<--- Score

26. Is there a control plan in place for sustaining improvements (short and long-term)?
<--- Score

27. Is there a standardized process?
<--- Score

28. What is the recommended frequency of auditing?
<--- Score

29. What other areas of the organization might benefit from the CGEIT team's improvements, knowledge, and learning?

<--- Score

30. Implementation Planning: is a pilot needed to test the changes before a full roll out occurs?
<--- Score

31. Does the CGEIT performance meet the customer's requirements?
<--- Score

32. Is there a recommended audit plan for routine surveillance inspections of CGEIT's gains?
<--- Score

33. Can you adapt and adjust to changing CGEIT situations?
<--- Score

34. How likely is the current CGEIT plan to come in on schedule or on budget?
<--- Score

35. You may have created your quality measures at a time when you lacked resources, technology wasn't up to the required standard, or low service levels were the industry norm. Have those circumstances changed?
<--- Score

36. Does CGEIT appropriately measure and monitor risk?
<--- Score

37. What do you measure to verify effectiveness gains?
<--- Score

38. Will your goals reflect your program budget?
<--- Score

39. How will the process owner verify improvement in present and future sigma levels, process capabilities?
<--- Score

40. What are the critical parameters to watch?
<--- Score

41. Against what alternative is success being measured?
<--- Score

42. Do the CGEIT decisions you make today help people and the planet tomorrow?
<--- Score

43. Are new process steps, standards, and documentation ingrained into normal operations?
<--- Score

44. Are documented procedures clear and easy to follow for the operators?
<--- Score

45. Do you monitor the CGEIT decisions made and fine tune them as they evolve?
<--- Score

46. Is new knowledge gained imbedded in the response plan?
<--- Score

47. What should the next improvement project be

that is related to CGEIT?
<--- Score

48. How do you plan on providing proper recognition and disclosure of supporting companies?
<--- Score

49. How will you measure your QA plan's effectiveness?
<--- Score

50. What are your results for key measures or indicators of the accomplishment of your CGEIT strategy and action plans, including building and strengthening core competencies?
<--- Score

51. Is a response plan established and deployed?
<--- Score

52. Are operating procedures consistent?
<--- Score

53. What is your theory of human motivation, and how does your compensation plan fit with that view?
<--- Score

54. How might the organization capture best practices and lessons learned so as to leverage improvements across the business?
<--- Score

55. What key inputs and outputs are being measured on an ongoing basis?
<--- Score

56. How will input, process, and output variables be checked to detect for sub-optimal conditions?
<--- Score

57. Will any special training be provided for results interpretation?
<--- Score

58. How do you select, collect, align, and integrate CGEIT data and information for tracking daily operations and overall organizational performance, including progress relative to strategic objectives and action plans?
<--- Score

59. How will new or emerging customer needs/requirements be checked/communicated to orient the process toward meeting the new specifications and continually reducing variation?
<--- Score

60. Are the planned controls in place?
<--- Score

61. What do you stand for--and what are you against?
<--- Score

62. How do controls support value?
<--- Score

63. Are suggested corrective/restorative actions indicated on the response plan for known causes to problems that might surface?
<--- Score

64. Are the planned controls working?

<--- Score

65. Who sets the CGEIT standards?
<--- Score

66. Will the team be available to assist members in planning investigations?
<--- Score

67. How will report readings be checked to effectively monitor performance?
<--- Score

68. What quality tools were useful in the control phase?
<--- Score

69. Who controls critical resources?
<--- Score

70. Are controls in place and consistently applied?
<--- Score

71. Who has control over resources?
<--- Score

72. Has the improved process and its steps been standardized?
<--- Score

73. Act/Adjust: What Do you Need to Do Differently?
<--- Score

74. Are you measuring, monitoring and predicting CGEIT activities to optimize operations and profitability, and enhancing outcomes?

<--- Score

75. Can support from partners be adjusted?
<--- Score

76. What do your reports reflect?
<--- Score

77. What adjustments to the strategies are needed?
<--- Score

78. Who will be in control?
<--- Score

79. How do you establish and deploy modified action plans if circumstances require a shift in plans and rapid execution of new plans?
<--- Score

80. How can you best use all of your knowledge repositories to enhance learning and sharing?
<--- Score

81. In the case of a CGEIT project, the criteria for the audit derive from implementation objectives. an audit of a CGEIT project involves assessing whether the recommendations outlined for implementation have been met. Can you track that any CGEIT project is implemented as planned, and is it working?
<--- Score

82. How do senior leaders actions reflect a commitment to the organizations CGEIT values?
<--- Score

83. How will the process owner and team be able to

hold the gains?
<--- Score

84. Is there a CGEIT Communication plan covering who needs to get what information when?
<--- Score

85. Are there documented procedures?
<--- Score

86. Do you monitor the effectiveness of your CGEIT activities?
<--- Score

87. Does job training on the documented procedures need to be part of the process team's education and training?
<--- Score

Add up total points for this section:
_ _ _ _ _ = Total points for this section

Divided by: _ _ _ _ _ _ (number of statements answered) = _ _ _ _ _ _
Average score for this section

Transfer your score to the CGEIT Index at the beginning of the Self-Assessment.

CRITERION #7: SUSTAIN:

INTENT: Retain the benefits.

In my belief, the answer to this question is clearly defined:

5 Strongly Agree

4 Agree

3 Neutral

2 Disagree

1 Strongly Disagree

1. Whom among your colleagues do you trust, and for what?
<--- Score

2. What is your competitive advantage?
<--- Score

3. What are the barriers to increased CGEIT production?
<--- Score

4. Who will manage the integration of tools?
<--- Score

5. What would have to be true for the option on the table to be the best possible choice?
<--- Score

6. How do you cross-sell and up-sell your CGEIT success?
<--- Score

7. What unique value proposition (UVP) do you offer?
<--- Score

8. What stupid rule would you most like to kill?
<--- Score

9. What is the range of capabilities?
<--- Score

10. What one word do you want to own in the minds of your customers, employees, and partners?
<--- Score

11. Did your employees make progress today?
<--- Score

12. How will you motivate the stakeholders with the least vested interest?
<--- Score

13. In retrospect, of the projects that you pulled the plug on, what percent do you wish had been allowed to keep going, and what percent do you wish had ended earlier?
<--- Score

14. If you got fired and a new hire took your place, what would she do different?
<--- Score

15. Is it economical; do you have the time and money?
<--- Score

16. How do you deal with CGEIT changes?
<--- Score

17. What are the responsibilities of Service Level Management?
<--- Score

18. How do you provide a safe environment -physically and emotionally?
<--- Score

19. How do you keep the momentum going?
<--- Score

20. Where do you start your DevOps transformation?
<--- Score

21. What are current CGEIT paradigms?
<--- Score

22. How do you manage performance of IT?
<--- Score

23. If you weren't already in this business, would you enter it today? And if not, what are you going to do about it?
<--- Score

24. If you were responsible for initiating and implementing major changes in your organization, what steps might you take to ensure acceptance of those changes?
<--- Score

25. What management system can you use to leverage the CGEIT experience, ideas, and concerns of the people closest to the work to be done?
<--- Score

26. Are the criteria for selecting recommendations stated?
<--- Score

27. Which models, tools and techniques are necessary?
<--- Score

28. Who do you think the world wants your organization to be?
<--- Score

29. How do you maintain CGEIT's Integrity?
<--- Score

30. Which are the advantages of IT Resource Management?
<--- Score

31. Would you rather sell to knowledgeable and informed customers or to uninformed customers?
<--- Score

32. What goals did you miss?

<--- Score

33. Is the CGEIT organization completing tasks effectively and efficiently?
<--- Score

34. Are you paying enough attention to the partners your company depends on to succeed?
<--- Score

35. Do you feel that more should be done in the CGEIT area?
<--- Score

36. Have benefits been optimized with all key stakeholders?
<--- Score

37. If you find that you havent accomplished one of the goals for one of the steps of the CGEIT strategy, what will you do to fix it?
<--- Score

38. How do you accomplish your long range CGEIT goals?
<--- Score

39. What type of cyber threats and vulnerabilities are you seeing?
<--- Score

40. Who is the main stakeholder, with ultimate responsibility for driving CGEIT forward?
<--- Score

41. What is the formula for measuring the usage

gap?
<--- Score

42. In a project to restructure CGEIT outcomes, which stakeholders would you involve?
<--- Score

43. What is the recommended frequency of auditing?
<--- Score

44. What are the usability implications of CGEIT actions?
<--- Score

45. Given your strategy, where should you spend your money?
<--- Score

46. Are you satisfied with your current role? If not, what is missing from it?
<--- Score

47. What are the rules and assumptions your industry operates under? What if the opposite were true?
<--- Score

48. Do CGEIT rules make a reasonable demand on a users capabilities?
<--- Score

49. Why do and why don't your customers like your organization?
<--- Score

50. What projects are going on in the organization today, and what resources are those projects using

from the resource pools?
<--- Score

51. To whom do you add value?
<--- Score

52. What are your personal philosophies regarding CGEIT and how do they influence your work?
<--- Score

53. Can the schedule be done in the given time?
<--- Score

54. How can you become more high-tech but still be high touch?
<--- Score

55. Which factors influence the operating environment of your enterprise?
<--- Score

56. What is your formula for success in CGEIT ?
<--- Score

57. Who will be responsible for deciding whether CGEIT goes ahead or not after the initial investigations?
<--- Score

58. Marketing budgets are tighter, consumers are more skeptical, and social media has changed forever the way we talk about CGEIT. How do you gain traction?
<--- Score

59. How do you go about securing CGEIT?

<--- Score

60. What is the kind of project structure that would be appropriate for your CGEIT project, should it be formal and complex, or can it be less formal and relatively simple?
<--- Score

61. Who have you, as a company, historically been when you've been at your best?
<--- Score

62. Has implementation been effective in reaching specified objectives so far?
<--- Score

63. What happens at your organization when people fail?
<--- Score

64. If no one would ever find out about your accomplishments, how would you lead differently?
<--- Score

65. How do you manage CGEIT Knowledge Management (KM)?
<--- Score

66. Which elements of Availability Management are used to perform at an agreed level over a period of time?
<--- Score

67. What is it like to work for you?
<--- Score

68. In the past year, what have you done (or could you have done) to increase the accurate perception of your company/brand as ethical and honest?
<--- Score

69. What should you stop doing?
<--- Score

70. What is the funding source for this project?
<--- Score

71. What happens when a new employee joins the organization?
<--- Score

72. What information is critical to your organization that your executives are ignoring?
<--- Score

73. Who else should you help?
<--- Score

74. What threat is CGEIT addressing?
<--- Score

75. What business benefits will CGEIT goals deliver if achieved?
<--- Score

76. Will there be any necessary staff changes (redundancies or new hires)?
<--- Score

77. Do you have an implicit bias for capital investments over people investments?
<--- Score

78. What are the business goals CGEIT is aiming to achieve?
<--- Score

79. Are you / should you be revolutionary or evolutionary?
<--- Score

80. What CGEIT skills are most important?
<--- Score

81. Is a CGEIT team work effort in place?
<--- Score

82. What are specific CGEIT rules to follow?
<--- Score

83. How are you doing compared to your industry?
<--- Score

84. What are the challenges?
<--- Score

85. Who will determine interim and final deadlines?
<--- Score

86. Do you think you know, or do you know you know ?
<--- Score

87. What are strategies for increasing support and reducing opposition?
<--- Score

88. How do you ensure that implementations of CGEIT

products are done in a way that ensures safety?
<--- Score

89. Does your organization have an IT Strategy or Steering Group which carries the overall accountability for setting governance, direction, policy and strategy for IT Services?
<--- Score

90. What CGEIT modifications can you make work for you?
<--- Score

91. Who do we want your customers to become?
<--- Score

92. What are the key enablers to make this CGEIT move?
<--- Score

93. What may be the consequences for the performance of an organization if all stakeholders are not consulted regarding CGEIT?
<--- Score

94. If there were zero limitations, what would you do differently?
<--- Score

95. How do you stay inspired?
<--- Score

96. How do you foster the skills, knowledge, talents, attributes, and characteristics you want to have?
<--- Score

97. How is business-IT alignment affected by a bimodal IT organization?
<--- Score

98. What is your BATNA (best alternative to a negotiated agreement)?
<--- Score

99. How will you ensure you get what you expected?
<--- Score

100. When information truly is ubiquitous, when reach and connectivity are completely global, when computing resources are infinite, and when a whole new set of impossibilities are not only possible, but happening, what will that do to your business?
<--- Score

101. Are you maintaining a past–present–future perspective throughout the CGEIT discussion?
<--- Score

102. Are you using a design thinking approach and integrating Innovation, CGEIT Experience, and Brand Value?
<--- Score

103. What are the potential basics of CGEIT fraud?
<--- Score

104. Who, on the executive team or the board, has spoken to a customer recently?
<--- Score

105. Is there any reason to believe the opposite of my current belief?

<--- Score

106. Why should you adopt a CGEIT framework?
<--- Score

107. Who are the key stakeholders?
<--- Score

108. Whose voice (department, ethnic group, women, older workers, etc) might you have missed hearing from in your company, and how might you amplify this voice to create positive momentum for your business?
<--- Score

109. Is there any existing CGEIT governance structure?
<--- Score

110. How can you become the company that would put you out of business?
<--- Score

111. Does IT support the enterprise in complying with regulations and service levels?
<--- Score

112. When you map the key players in your own work and the types/domains of relationships with them, which relationships do you find easy and which challenging, and why?
<--- Score

113. Is there a work around that you can use?
<--- Score

114. Ask yourself: how would you do this work if you

only had one staff member to do it?
<--- Score

115. Do you have the right people on the bus?
<--- Score

116. How do you create buy-in?
<--- Score

117. What trouble can you get into?
<--- Score

118. What does your signature ensure?
<--- Score

119. Can you do all this work?
<--- Score

120. Is maximizing CGEIT protection the same as minimizing CGEIT loss?
<--- Score

121. What is a feasible sequencing of reform initiatives over time?
<--- Score

122. Why is it important to have a strategic fit between the companies involved in a buyer/seller alliance or partnership?
<--- Score

123. How can you incorporate support to ensure safe and effective use of CGEIT into the services that you provide?
<--- Score

124. How do you keep records, of what?
<--- Score

125. What does strategic IT really consist of?
<--- Score

126. Who is responsible for ensuring appropriate resources (time, people and money) are allocated to CGEIT?
<--- Score

127. If you had to leave your organization for a year and the only communication you could have with employees/colleagues was a single paragraph, what would you write?
<--- Score

128. What is the overall business strategy?
<--- Score

129. Will it be accepted by users?
<--- Score

130. How do customers see your organization?
<--- Score

131. What are the short and long-term CGEIT goals?
<--- Score

132. What safeguards are available?
<--- Score

133. What is your question? Why?
<--- Score

134. What knowledge, skills and characteristics mark a

good CGEIT project manager?
<--- Score

135. How does it align with to the to be architecture?
<--- Score

136. How do you know if you are successful?
<--- Score

137. How do you listen to customers to obtain actionable information?
<--- Score

138. What do we do when new problems arise?
<--- Score

139. Why is CGEIT important for you now?
<--- Score

140. What have been your experiences in defining long range CGEIT goals?
<--- Score

141. Are you making progress, and are you making progress as CGEIT leaders?
<--- Score

142. Are new benefits received and understood?
<--- Score

143. Why should people listen to you?
<--- Score

144. Instead of going to current contacts for new ideas, what if you reconnected with dormant

contacts--the people you used to know? If you were going reactivate a dormant tie, who would it be?
<--- Score

145. Is there a regulatory role in the implementation of the framework?
<--- Score

146. How important is CGEIT to the user organizations mission?
<--- Score

147. What is the craziest thing you can do?
<--- Score

148. Is CGEIT dependent on the successful delivery of a current project?
<--- Score

149. What are the gaps in your knowledge and experience?
<--- Score

150. Do you have enough freaky customers in your portfolio pushing you to the limit day in and day out?
<--- Score

151. Who uses your product in ways you never expected?
<--- Score

152. How do you know the enterprise is compliant with applicable rules and regulations?
<--- Score

153. Strategic alignment: How well does the IT

investment strategy align with the long-term goals of the business?
<--- Score

154. Do you see more potential in people than they do in themselves?
<--- Score

155. Operational - will it work?
<--- Score

156. What role does communication play in the success or failure of a CGEIT project?
<--- Score

157. What counts that you are not counting?
<--- Score

158. How do you get value from the use of IT?
<--- Score

159. How is implementation research currently incorporated into each of your goals?
<--- Score

160. How do you make it meaningful in connecting CGEIT with what users do day-to-day?
<--- Score

161. How does CGEIT integrate with other business initiatives?
<--- Score

162. What would you recommend your friend do if he/she were facing this dilemma?
<--- Score

163. How do alignment and information sharing influence the operational performance of your organization?
<--- Score

164. What is effective CGEIT?
<--- Score

165. Is CGEIT realistic, or are you setting yourself up for failure?
<--- Score

166. What will be the consequences to the stakeholder (financial, reputation etc) if CGEIT does not go ahead or fails to deliver the objectives?
<--- Score

167. Is the impact that CGEIT has shown?
<--- Score

168. How do you transition from the baseline to the target?
<--- Score

169. What is something you believe that nearly no one agrees with you on?
<--- Score

170. If you do not follow, then how to lead?
<--- Score

171. What are the essentials of internal CGEIT management?
<--- Score

172. Political -is anyone trying to undermine this project?
<--- Score

173. How much does CGEIT help?
<--- Score

174. Is your strategy driving your strategy? Or is the way in which you allocate resources driving your strategy?
<--- Score

175. Who will provide the final approval of CGEIT deliverables?
<--- Score

176. Do you have the right capabilities and capacities?
<--- Score

177. What are the success criteria that will indicate that CGEIT objectives have been met and the benefits delivered?
<--- Score

178. What are the top 3 things at the forefront of your CGEIT agendas for the next 3 years?
<--- Score

179. How will you insure seamless interoperability of CGEIT moving forward?
<--- Score

180. What potential megatrends could make your business model obsolete?
<--- Score

181. What are internal and external CGEIT relations?
<--- Score

182. Why will customers want to buy your organizations products/services?
<--- Score

183. How long will it take to change?
<--- Score

184. Who is on the team?
<--- Score

185. How can you negotiate CGEIT successfully with a stubborn boss, an irate client, or a deceitful coworker?
<--- Score

186. Who do you want your customers to become?
<--- Score

187. Can you maintain your growth without detracting from the factors that have contributed to your success?
<--- Score

188. How do you lead with CGEIT in mind?
<--- Score

189. Why is it important to have senior management support for a CGEIT project?
<--- Score

190. Who are your customers?
<--- Score

191. Do you have enough people for IT?

<--- Score

192. What kind of crime could a potential new hire have committed that would not only not disqualify him/her from being hired by your organization, but would actually indicate that he/she might be a particularly good fit?
<--- Score

193. Are there any activities that you can take off your to do list?
<--- Score

194. Are assumptions made in CGEIT stated explicitly?
<--- Score

195. Have new benefits been realized?
<--- Score

196. Are all key stakeholders present at all Structured Walkthroughs?
<--- Score

197. Which functions and people interact with the supplier and or customer?
<--- Score

198. What was the last experiment you ran?
<--- Score

199. What happens if you do not have enough funding?
<--- Score

200. Which areas addresses the safeguarding of IT assets, disaster recovery and continuity of

operations?
<--- Score

201. What are you trying to prove to yourself, and how might it be hijacking your life and business success?
<--- Score

202. What new services of functionality will be implemented next with CGEIT ?
<--- Score

203. Which CGEIT goals are the most important?
<--- Score

204. What is the purpose of CGEIT in relation to the mission?
<--- Score

205. What you are going to do to affect the numbers?
<--- Score

206. How do you assess the CGEIT pitfalls that are inherent in implementing it?
<--- Score

207. How have changes in your business model and/or strategic initiatives increased vulnerabilities?
<--- Score

208. What relationships among CGEIT trends do you perceive?
<--- Score

209. Do you know what you are doing? And who do you call if you don't?

<--- Score

210. What is the overall talent health of your organization as a whole at senior levels, and for each organization reporting to a member of the Senior Leadership Team?
<--- Score

211. How do you govern and fulfill your societal responsibilities?
<--- Score

212. Where can you break convention?
<--- Score

213. Do you have past CGEIT successes?
<--- Score

214. How do you track customer value, profitability or financial return, organizational success, and sustainability?
<--- Score

215. How do you set CGEIT stretch targets and how do you get people to not only participate in setting these stretch targets but also that they strive to achieve these?
<--- Score

216. If you had to rebuild your organization without any traditional competitive advantages (i.e., no killer a technology, promising research, innovative product/ service delivery model, etc.), how would your people have to approach their work and collaborate together in order to create the necessary conditions for success?

<--- Score

217. How do users view the IT department?
<--- Score

218. Who is responsible for CGEIT?
<--- Score

219. Is your basic point _____ or _____?
<--- Score

220. What trophy do you want on your mantle?
<--- Score

221. What are the long-term CGEIT goals?
<--- Score

222. How does management view the IT department?
<--- Score

223. Are your responses positive or negative?
<--- Score

224. Are there any disadvantages to implementing CGEIT? There might be some that are less obvious?
<--- Score

225. What are your most important goals for the strategic CGEIT objectives?
<--- Score

226. Who are four people whose careers you have enhanced?
<--- Score

227. Can you break it down?
<--- Score

228. How will you know that the CGEIT project has been successful?
<--- Score

229. What is the source of the strategies for CGEIT strengthening and reform?
<--- Score

230. What is the estimated value of the project?
<--- Score

231. Are you relevant? Will you be relevant five years from now? Ten?
<--- Score

232. Were lessons learned captured and communicated?
<--- Score

233. Are you changing as fast as the world around you?
<--- Score

234. If your company went out of business tomorrow, would anyone who doesn't get a paycheck here care?
<--- Score

235. What is an unauthorized commitment?
<--- Score

236. How do you foster innovation?
<--- Score

237. Which individuals, teams or departments will be involved in CGEIT?
<--- Score

238. Think of your CGEIT project, what are the main functions?
<--- Score

239. How much contingency will be available in the budget?
<--- Score

240. What is your CGEIT strategy?
<--- Score

241. Why not do CGEIT?
<--- Score

242. Do you think CGEIT accomplishes the goals you expect it to accomplish?
<--- Score

243. What are you challenging?
<--- Score

244. At what moment would you think; Will I get fired?
<--- Score

245. How do you proactively clarify deliverables and CGEIT quality expectations?
<--- Score

246. Who is responsible for errors?
<--- Score

247. How do you engage the workforce, in addition to

satisfying them?
<--- Score

248. Are the assumptions believable and achievable?
<--- Score

249. What must you excel at?
<--- Score

250. How do senior leaders deploy your organizations vision and values through your leadership system, to the workforce, to key suppliers and partners, and to customers and other stakeholders, as appropriate?
<--- Score

251. How do you determine the key elements that affect CGEIT workforce satisfaction, how are these elements determined for different workforce groups and segments?
<--- Score

252. What have you done to protect your business from competitive encroachment?
<--- Score

253. How critical is IT to sustaining the enterprise?
<--- Score

254. Which are the objectives of Service Level Management (SLM)?
<--- Score

255. If your customer were your grandmother, would you tell her to buy what you're selling?
<--- Score

256. Do you say no to customers for no reason?
<--- Score

257. What did you miss in the interview for the worst hire you ever made?
<--- Score

258. How likely is it that a customer would recommend your company to a friend or colleague?
<--- Score

Add up total points for this section:
_____ = Total points for this section

Divided by: _____ (number of statements answered) = _____
Average score for this section

Transfer your score to the CGEIT Index at the beginning of the Self-Assessment.

CGEIT and Managing Projects, Criteria for Project Managers:

1.0 Initiating Process Group: CGEIT

1. What will be the pressing issues of tomorrow?

2. Do you know all the stakeholders impacted by the CGEIT project and what needs are?

3. Does the CGEIT project team have enough people to execute the CGEIT project plan?

4. Have the stakeholders identified all individual requirements pertaining to business process?

5. How can you make your needs known?

6. The process to Manage Stakeholders is part of which process group?

7. Mitigate. what will you do to minimize the impact should the risk event occur?

8. Specific - is the objective clear in terms of what, how, when, and where the situation will be changed?

9. How will you know you did it?

10. What input will you be required to provide the CGEIT project team?

11. Were decisions made in a timely manner?

12. How to control and approve each phase?

13. What communication items need improvement?

14. Are the CGEIT project team and stakeholders meeting regularly and using a meeting agenda and taking notes to accurately document what is being covered and what happened in the weekly meetings?

15. Have you evaluated the teams performance and asked for feedback?

16. Are there resources to maintain and support the outcome of the CGEIT project?

17. For technology CGEIT projects only: Are all production support stakeholders (Business unit, technical support, & user) prepared for implementation with appropriate contingency plans?

18. What are the overarching issues of your organization?

19. What is the stake of others in your CGEIT project?

20. What is the NEXT thing to do?

1.1 Project Charter: CGEIT

21. What is the business need?

22. How much?

23. Why is a CGEIT project Charter used?

24. How are CGEIT projects different from operations?

25. When will this occur?

26. What are the deliverables?

27. What are some examples of a business case?

28. When do you use a CGEIT project Charter?

29. Is it an improvement over existing products?

30. Whose input and support will this CGEIT project require?

31. What are the assigned resources?

32. Strategic fit: what is the strategic initiative identifier for this CGEIT project?

33. What are the known stakeholder requirements?

34. Why use a CGEIT project charter?

35. What is the purpose of the CGEIT project?

36. Name and describe the elements that deal with providing the detail?

37. What is the most common tool for helping define the detail?

38. Assumptions and constraints: what assumptions were made in defining the CGEIT project?

39. Where and how does the team fit within your organization structure?

40. Did your CGEIT project ask for this?

1.2 Stakeholder Register: CGEIT

41. How much influence do they have on the CGEIT project?

42. Who is managing stakeholder engagement?

43. Who are the stakeholders?

44. How will reports be created?

45. Who wants to talk about Security?

46. What & Why?

47. How big is the gap?

48. What are the major CGEIT project milestones requiring communications or providing communications opportunities?

49. How should employers make voices heard?

50. What is the power of the stakeholder?

51. Is your organization ready for change?

52. What opportunities exist to provide communications?

1.3 Stakeholder Analysis Matrix: CGEIT

53. How to measure the achievement of the Outputs?

54. What could your organization improve?

55. Does your organization have bad debt or cash-flow problems?

56. What can the stakeholder prevent from happening?

57. What is your organizations competitors doing?

58. What is your Risk Management?

59. Are the interests in line with the program objectives?

60. Will the impacts be local, national or international?

61. Competitors vulnerabilities?

62. Timescales, deadlines and pressures?

63. Usps (unique selling points)?

64. What is your Advocacy Strategy?

65. Legislative effects?

66. New technologies, services, ideas?

67. Alliances: with which other actors is the actor allied, how are they interconnected?

68. Price, value, quality?

69. Cashflow, start-up cash-drain?

70. Why do you care?

71. Do any safeguard policies apply to the CGEIT project?

72. Continuity, supply chain robustness?

2.0 Planning Process Group: CGEIT

73. Who are the CGEIT project stakeholders?

74. If action is called for, what form should it take?

75. Is the duration of the program sufficient to ensure a cycle that will CGEIT project the sustainability of the interventions?

76. When will the CGEIT project be done?

77. Does it make any difference if you are successful?

78. Why is it important to determine activity sequencing on CGEIT projects?

79. How well defined and documented are the CGEIT project management processes you chose to use?

80. When developing the estimates for CGEIT project phases, you choose to add the individual estimates for the activities that comprise each phase. What type of estimation method are you using?

81. What factors are contributing to progress or delay in the achievement of products and results?

82. Is the CGEIT project supported by national and/or local organizations?

83. In what ways can the governance of the CGEIT project be improved so that it has greater likelihood of achieving future sustainability?

84. What good practices or successful experiences or transferable examples have been identified?

85. In which CGEIT project management process group is the detailed CGEIT project budget created?

86. Have operating capacities been created and/or reinforced in partners?

87. In what way has the program contributed towards the issue culture and development included on the public agenda?

88. Are work methodologies, financial instruments, etc. shared among departments, organizations and CGEIT projects?

89. To what extent are the visions and actions of the partners consistent or divergent with regard to the program?

90. How well did the chosen processes fit the needs of the CGEIT project?

91. How can you tell when you are done?

92. How will it affect you?

2.1 Project Management Plan: CGEIT

93. Why do you manage integration?

94. What should you drop in order to add something new?

95. How do you manage integration?

96. Has the selected plan been formulated using cost effectiveness and incremental analysis techniques?

97. What data/reports/tools/etc. do your PMs need?

98. Who is the CGEIT project Manager?

99. What is CGEIT project scope management?

100. Is the engineering content at a feasibility level-of-detail, and is it sufficiently complete, to provide an adequate basis for the baseline cost estimate?

101. How can you best help your organization to develop consistent practices in CGEIT project management planning stages?

102. Are calculations and results of analyzes essentially correct?

103. What if, for example, the positive direction and vision of your organization causes expected trends to change resulting in greater need than expected?

104. Who is the sponsor?

105. How well are you able to manage your risk?

106. How do you organize the costs in the CGEIT project management plan?

107. What data/reports/tools/etc. do program managers need?

108. What would you do differently what did not work?

109. If the CGEIT project is complex or scope is specialized, do you have appropriate and/or qualified staff available to perform the tasks?

2.2 Scope Management Plan: CGEIT

110. Is quality monitored from the perspective of the customers needs and expectations?

111. Does the resource management plan include a personnel development plan?

112. Have reserves been created to address risks?

113. What do you need to do to accomplish the goal or goals?

114. How do you plan to control Scope Creep?

115. Are vendor invoices audited for accuracy before payment?

116. Have all necessary approvals been obtained?

117. Are decisions captured in a decisions log?

118. During what part of the PM process is the CGEIT project scope statement created?

119. Is the assigned CGEIT project manager a PMP (Certified CGEIT project manager) and experienced?

120. Is stakeholder involvement adequate?

121. Are actuals compared against estimates to analyze and correct variances?

122. What are the risks that could significantly affect

the scope of the CGEIT project?

123. Pareto diagrams, statistical sampling, flow charting or trend analysis used quality monitoring?

124. Staffing Requirements?

125. Will the CGEIT project deliverables become accepted in writing?

126. Will anyone else be involved in verifying the deliverables?

127. Has a capability assessment been conducted?

128. Does the CGEIT project have a Quality Culture?

129. How many changes are you making?

2.3 Requirements Management Plan: CGEIT

130. How will you develop the schedule of requirements activities?

131. Is the change control process documented?

132. Is the user satisfied?

133. Should you include sub-activities?

134. What performance metrics will be used?

135. Is the system software (non-operating system) new to the IT CGEIT project team?

136. Who will perform the analysis?

137. Did you provide clear and concise specifications?

138. Does the CGEIT project have a Change Control process?

139. Has the requirements team been instructed in the Change Control process?

140. Do you really need to write this document at all?

141. How often will the reporting occur?

142. What went wrong?

143. Who came up with this requirement?

144. How knowledgeable is the team in the proposed application area?

145. Is any organizational data being used or stored?

146. Will the product release be stable and mature enough to be deployed in the user community?

147. Who will approve the requirements (and if multiple approvers, in what order)?

148. Did you distinguish the scope of work the contractor(s) will be required to do?

149. Did you avoid subjective, flowery or non-specific statements?

2.4 Requirements Documentation: CGEIT

150. How can you document system requirements?

151. Who provides requirements?

152. What can tools do for us?

153. Have the benefits identified with the system being identified clearly?

154. Is the requirement realistically testable?

155. How much testing do you need to do to prove that your system is safe?

156. Is the requirement properly understood?

157. What is your Elevator Speech?

158. What if the system wasn t implemented?

159. Does your organization restrict technical alternatives?

160. Can you check system requirements?

161. How linear / iterative is your Requirements Gathering process (or will it be)?

162. What are the acceptance criteria?

163. How will they be documented / shared?

164. How much does requirements engineering cost?

165. Can the requirements be checked?

166. Who is interacting with the system?

167. What is a show stopper in the requirements?

168. Do technical resources exist?

2.5 Requirements Traceability Matrix: CGEIT

169. What is the WBS?

170. What percentage of CGEIT projects are producing traceability matrices between requirements and other work products?

171. Why do you manage scope?

172. Do you have a clear understanding of all subcontracts in place?

173. How small is small enough?

174. How will it affect the stakeholders personally in their career?

175. Is there a requirements traceability process in place?

176. Will you use a Requirements Traceability Matrix?

177. Describe the process for approving requirements so they can be added to the traceability matrix and CGEIT project work can be performed. Will the CGEIT project requirements become approved in writing?

178. Why use a WBS?

179. How do you manage scope?

180. What are the chronologies, contingencies, consequences, criteria?

2.6 Project Scope Statement: CGEIT

181. Change management vs. change leadership - what is the difference?

182. How often will scope changes be reviewed?

183. Which risks does the CGEIT project focus on?

184. Is the plan for your organization of the CGEIT project resources adequate?

185. Are there adequate CGEIT project control systems?

186. If the scope changes, what will the impact be to your CGEIT project in terms of duration, cost, quality, or any other important areas of the CGEIT project?

187. Once its defined, what is the stability of the CGEIT project scope?

188. What actions will be taken to mitigate the risk?

189. Will the risk status be reported to management on a regular and frequent basis?

190. Will statistics related to QA be collected, trends analyzed, and problems raised as issues?

191. Any new risks introduced or old risks impacted. Are there issues that could affect the existing requirements for the result, service, or product if the scope changes?

192. Were potential customers involved early in the planning process?

193. How will you haverify the accuracy of the work of the CGEIT project, and what constitutes acceptance of the deliverables?

194. Does the scope statement still need some clarity?

195. Is the CGEIT project manager qualified and experienced in CGEIT project management?

196. Will the qa related information be reported regularly as part of the status reporting mechanisms?

197. Is the plan for CGEIT project resources adequate?

198. Identify how your team and you will create the CGEIT project scope statement and the work breakdown structure (WBS). Document how you will create the CGEIT project scope statement and WBS, and make sure you answer the following questions: In defining CGEIT project scope and the WBS, will you and your CGEIT project team be using methods defined by your organization, methods defined by the CGEIT project management office (PMO), or other methods?

199. Is there a Quality Assurance Plan documented and filed?

2.7 Assumption and Constraint Log: CGEIT

200. Can the requirements be traced to the appropriate components of the solution, as well as test scripts?

201. Does the system design reflect the requirements?

202. What worked well?

203. Do the requirements meet the standards of correctness, completeness, consistency, accuracy, and readability?

204. What do you log?

205. Have CGEIT project management standards and procedures been established and documented?

206. Would known impacts serve as impediments?

207. Is the process working, and people are not executing in compliance of the process?

208. Are formal code reviews conducted?

209. Are requirements management tracking tools and procedures in place?

210. If it is out of compliance, should the process be amended or should the Plan be amended?

211. Does the traceability documentation describe the tool and/or mechanism to be used to capture traceability throughout the life cycle?

212. Are there procedures in place to effectively manage interdependencies with other CGEIT projects / systems?

213. How are new requirements or changes to requirements identified?

214. What weaknesses do you have?

215. After observing execution of process, is it in compliance with the documented Plan?

216. Has the approach and development strategy of the CGEIT project been defined, documented and accepted by the appropriate stakeholders?

217. What if failure during recovery?

218. What do you audit?

219. Are there cosmetic errors that hinder readability and comprehension?

2.8 Work Breakdown Structure: CGEIT

220. What has to be done?

221. How will you and your CGEIT project team define the CGEIT projects scope and work breakdown structure?

222. Where does it take place?

223. Do you need another level?

224. How far down?

225. When would you develop a Work Breakdown Structure?

226. What is the probability that the CGEIT project duration will exceed xx weeks?

227. Can you make it?

228. How many levels?

229. Why would you develop a Work Breakdown Structure?

230. Is it a change in scope?

231. Is the work breakdown structure (wbs) defined and is the scope of the CGEIT project clear with assigned deliverable owners?

232. When do you stop?

233. Is it still viable?

234. How big is a work-package?

235. When does it have to be done?

236. Why is it useful?

237. Who has to do it?

238. What is the probability of completing the CGEIT project in less that xx days?

239. How much detail?

2.9 WBS Dictionary: CGEIT

240. The anticipated business volume?

241. Time-phased control account budgets?

242. Are work packages reasonably short in time duration or do they have adequate objective indicators/milestones to minimize subjectivity of the in process work evaluation?

243. All cwbs elements specified for external reporting?

244. Detailed schedules which support control account and work package start and completion dates/events?

245. Are overhead budgets and costs being handled according to the disclosure statement when applicable, or otherwise properly classified (for example, engineering overhead, IR&D)?

246. Does the contractors system identify work accomplishment against the schedule plan?

247. Are overhead cost budgets established for each organization which has authority to incur overhead costs?

248. Appropriate work authorization documents which subdivide the contractual effort and responsibilities, within functional organizations?

249. The total budget for the contract (including estimates for authorized and unpriced work)?

250. Are the contractors estimates of costs at completion reconcilable with cost data reported to us?

251. Are overhead cost budgets (or CGEIT projections) established on a facility-wide basis at least annually for the life of the contract?

252. Does the contractors system include procedures for measuring the performance of critical subcontractors?

253. The CGEIT projected business base for each period?

254. Does the contractors system description or procedures require that the performance measurement baseline plus management reserve equal the contract budget base?

255. Are internal budgets for authorized, and not priced changes based on the contractors resource plan for accomplishing the work?

256. Are retroactive changes to direct costs and indirect costs prohibited except for the correction of errors and routine accounting adjustments?

257. Does the contractors system provide unit or lot costs when applicable?

258. Is data disseminated to the contractors management timely, accurate, and usable?

2.10 Schedule Management Plan: CGEIT

259. Which status reports are received per the CGEIT project Plan?

260. Have the key functions and capabilities been defined and assigned to each release or iteration?

261. Have CGEIT project management standards and procedures been identified / established and documented?

262. Is the quality assurance team identified?

263. Is the critical path valid?

264. Is there a set of procedures defining the scope, procedures, and deliverables defining quality control?

265. Are assumptions being identified, recorded, analyzed, qualified and closed?

266. Quality assurance overheads?

267. Is a process defined for baseline approval and control?

268. After initial schedule development, will the schedule be reviewed and validated by the CGEIT project team?

269. Is pert / critical path or equivalent methodology

being used?

270. Is funded schedule margin reasonable and logically distributed?

271. Are milestone deliverables effectively tracked and compared to CGEIT project plan?

272. Is CGEIT project status reviewed with the steering and executive teams at appropriate intervals?

273. Are estimating assumptions and constraints captured?

274. Is the schedule updated on a periodic basis?

275. Are the predecessor and successor relationships accurate?

276. What date will the task finish?

2.11 Activity List: CGEIT

277. When do the individual activities need to start and finish?

278. What is the probability the CGEIT project can be completed in xx weeks?

279. What are you counting on?

280. In what sequence?

281. What went right?

282. Is infrastructure setup part of your CGEIT project?

283. How should ongoing costs be monitored to try to keep the CGEIT project within budget?

284. How can the CGEIT project be displayed graphically to better visualize the activities?

285. Are the required resources available or need to be acquired?

286. How difficult will it be to do specific activities on this CGEIT project?

287. Who will perform the work?

288. What is the LF and LS for each activity?

289. Can you determine the activity that must finish, before this activity can start?

290. The wbs is developed as part of a joint planning session. and how do you know that youhave done this right?

291. How will it be performed?

292. Is there anything planned that does not need to be here?

293. What will be performed?

294. How much slack is available in the CGEIT project?

2.12 Activity Attributes: CGEIT

295. Activity: fair or not fair?

296. What is your organizations history in doing similar activities?

297. What conclusions/generalizations can you draw from this?

298. Which method produces the more accurate cost assignment?

299. Why?

300. How do you manage time?

301. Activity: what is Missing?

302. Can you re-assign any activities to another resource to resolve an over-allocation?

303. Resource is assigned to?

304. Is there a trend during the year?

305. Time for overtime?

306. What is missing?

307. Activity: what is In the Bag?

308. What activity do you think you should spend the most time on?

309. How many resources do you need to complete the work scope within a limit of X number of days?

310. What is the general pattern here?

311. Are the required resources available?

312. Were there other ways you could have organized the data to achieve similar results?

2.13 Milestone List: CGEIT

313. How late can the activity finish?

314. Sustaining internal capabilities?

315. What has been done so far?

316. Obstacles faced?

317. New USPs?

318. Vital contracts and partners?

319. Marketing - reach, distribution, awareness?

320. Political effects?

321. Competitive advantages?

322. Who will manage the CGEIT project on a day-to-day basis?

323. Sustainable financial backing?

324. Environmental effects?

325. Milestone pages should display the UserID of the person who added the milestone. Does a report or query exist that provides this audit information?

326. Reliability of data, plan predictability?

327. Describe the industry you are in and the market

growth opportunities. What is the market for your technology, product or service?

328. What specific improvements did you make to the CGEIT project proposal since the previous time?

329. Identify critical paths (one or more) and which activities are on the critical path?

330. When will the CGEIT project be complete?

331. Own known vulnerabilities?

2.14 Network Diagram: CGEIT

332. What job or jobs follow it?

333. What are the Key Success Factors?

334. Exercise: what is the probability that the CGEIT project duration will exceed xx weeks?

335. If a current contract exists, can you provide the vendor name, contract start, and contract expiration date?

336. What to do and When?

337. What is the probability of completing the CGEIT project in less that xx days?

338. Where do you schedule uncertainty time?

339. What job or jobs could run concurrently?

340. How difficult will it be to do specific activities on this CGEIT project?

341. What is the completion time?

342. What are the tools?

343. What is the lowest cost to complete this CGEIT project in xx weeks?

344. Are the gantt chart and/or network diagram updated periodically and used to assess the overall

CGEIT project timetable?

345. What activities must follow this activity?

346. Review the logical flow of the network diagram. Take a look at which activities you have first and then sequence the activities. Do they make sense?

347. How confident can you be in your milestone dates and the delivery date?

348. What can be done concurrently?

349. What are the Major Administrative Issues?

350. Why must you schedule milestones, such as reviews, throughout the CGEIT project?

2.15 Activity Resource Requirements: CGEIT

351. When does monitoring begin?

352. Which logical relationship does the PDM use most often?

353. Other support in specific areas?

354. Do you use tools like decomposition and rolling-wave planning to produce the activity list and other outputs?

355. Organizational Applicability?

356. Anything else?

357. Are there unresolved issues that need to be addressed?

358. Why do you do that?

359. How many signatures do you require on a check and does this match what is in your policy and procedures?

360. What is the Work Plan Standard?

361. How do you handle petty cash?

362. What are constraints that you might find during the Human Resource Planning process?

2.16 Resource Breakdown Structure: CGEIT

363. What is the purpose of assigning and documenting responsibility?

364. Why do you do it?

365. What is the difference between % Complete and % work?

366. Who will be used as a CGEIT project team member?

367. How difficult will it be to do specific activities on this CGEIT project?

368. What are the requirements for resource data?

369. Which resource planning tool provides information on resource responsibility and accountability?

370. Who needs what information?

371. Why is this important?

372. Changes based on input from stakeholders?

373. What is each stakeholders desired outcome for the CGEIT project?

374. How should the information be delivered?

375. Who is allowed to perform which functions?

376. What is CGEIT project communication management?

377. How can this help you with team building?

378. Why time management?

2.17 Activity Duration Estimates: CGEIT

379. Why is there a new or renewed interest in the field of CGEIT project management?

380. How do functionality, system outputs, performance, reliability, and maintainability requirements affect quality planning?

381. How does CGEIT project management relate to other disciplines?

382. What are crucial elements of successful CGEIT project plan execution?

383. Will the new application be developed using existing hardware, software, and networks?

384. What are the main parts of a scope statement?

385. Total slack can be calculated by which equations?

386. What functions does this software provide that cannot be done easily using other tools such as a spreadsheet or database?

387. What is the difference between conceptual, application, and evaluative questions?

388. Does a process exist to determine the potential loss or gain if risk events occur?

389. What tasks must precede this task?

390. Do checklists exist that list frequently performed activities?

391. Sigma CGEIT project?

392. (Cpi), and schedule performance index (spi) for the CGEIT project?

393. Who has the PRIMARY responsibility to solve this problem?

394. What are some general rules of thumb for deciding if cost variance, schedule variance, cost performance index, and schedule performance index numbers are good or bad?

395. Do you think CGEIT project managers of large information technology CGEIT projects need strong technical skills?

2.18 Duration Estimating Worksheet: CGEIT

396. What utility impacts are there?

397. Define the work as completely as possible. What work will be included in the CGEIT project?

398. Science = process: remember the scientific method?

399. What is an Average CGEIT project?

400. What info is needed?

401. What work will be included in the CGEIT project?

402. Why estimate time and cost?

403. When does your organization expect to be able to complete it?

404. How can the CGEIT project be displayed graphically to better visualize the activities?

405. Why estimate costs?

406. What is next?

407. Is a construction detail attached (to aid in explanation)?

408. What is your role?

409. When, then?

410. Does the CGEIT project provide innovative ways for stakeholders to overcome obstacles or deliver better outcomes?

411. Is this operation cost effective?

412. What is the total time required to complete the CGEIT project if no delays occur?

413. Is the CGEIT project responsive to community need?

2.19 Project Schedule: CGEIT

414. Understand the constraints used in preparing the schedule. Are activities connected because logic dictates the order in which others occur?

415. What is the purpose of a CGEIT project schedule?

416. How do you use schedules?

417. Should you have a test for each code module?

418. What is CGEIT project management?

419. Was the CGEIT project schedule reviewed by all stakeholders and formally accepted?

420. Why do you think schedule issues often cause the most conflicts on CGEIT projects?

421. What is risk management?

422. Does the condition or event threaten the CGEIT projects objectives in any ways?

423. Why is software CGEIT project disaster so common?

424. How can you minimize or control changes to CGEIT project schedules?

425. How do you manage CGEIT project Risk?

426. Master CGEIT project schedule?

427. Did the final product meet or exceed user expectations?

428. It allows the CGEIT project to be delivered on schedule. How Do you Use Schedules?

429. Why is this particularly bad?

2.20 Cost Management Plan: CGEIT

430. Are enough systems & user personnel assigned to the CGEIT project?

431. Risk rating?

432. What are the nine areas of expertise?

433. Was the CGEIT project schedule reviewed by all stakeholders and formally accepted?

434. Is a pmo (CGEIT project management office) in place and provide oversight to the CGEIT project?

435. Best practices implementation – How will change management be applied to this CGEIT project?

436. Is there an on-going process in place to monitor CGEIT project risks?

437. Is a stakeholder management plan in place that covers topics?

438. Escalation criteria met?

439. Forecasts – how will the time and resources needed to complete the CGEIT project be forecast?

440. Are all vendor contracts closed out?

441. Are key risk mitigation strategies added to the CGEIT project schedule?

442. What is your organizations history in doing similar tasks?

443. Is there an onboarding process in place?

444. Are the appropriate IT resources adequate to meet planned commitments?

445. Will the forecasts be based on trend analysis and earned value statistics?

446. Are the key elements of a CGEIT project Charter present?

447. Are all resource assumptions documented?

2.21 Activity Cost Estimates: CGEIT

448. Did the consultant work with local staff to develop local capacity?

449. Does the activity rely on a common set of tools to carry it out?

450. Does the estimator have experience?

451. Were escalated issues resolved promptly?

452. What is included in indirect cost being allocated?

453. Were sponsors and decision makers available when needed outside regularly scheduled meetings?

454. What defines a successful CGEIT project?

455. Performance bond should always provide what part of the contract value?

456. Will you need to provide essential services information about activities?

457. What is a CGEIT project Management Plan?

458. How Award?

459. Is costing method consistent with study goals?

460. Were you satisfied with the work?

461. What makes a good expected result statement?

462. Scope statement only direct or indirect costs as well?

463. How many activities should you have?

464. Who determines the quality and expertise of contractors?

465. How do you change activities?

2.22 Cost Estimating Worksheet: CGEIT

466. Who is best positioned to know and assist in identifying corresponding factors?

467. What is the estimated labor cost today based upon this information?

468. Value pocket identification & quantification what are value pockets?

469. What additional CGEIT project(s) could be initiated as a result of this CGEIT project?

470. What costs are to be estimated?

471. Ask: are others positioned to know, are others credible, and will others cooperate?

472. Is it feasible to establish a control group arrangement?

473. Will the CGEIT project collaborate with the local community and leverage resources?

474. What can be included?

475. Can a trend be established from historical performance data on the selected measure and are the criteria for using trend analysis or forecasting methods met?

476. What will others want?

477. Is the CGEIT project responsive to community need?

478. How will the results be shared and to whom?

479. Identify the timeframe necessary to monitor progress and collect data to determine how the selected measure has changed?

480. What is the purpose of estimating?

481. What happens to any remaining funds not used?

482. Does the CGEIT project provide innovative ways for stakeholders to overcome obstacles or deliver better outcomes?

2.23 Cost Baseline: CGEIT

483. Is request in line with priorities?

484. Verify business objectives. Are others appropriate, and well-articulated?

485. What is the most important thing to do next to make your CGEIT project successful?

486. For what purpose ?

487. What can go wrong?

488. Pcs for your new business. what would the life cycle costs be?

489. Eac -estimate at completion, what is the total job expected to cost?

490. Does a process exist for establishing a cost baseline to measure CGEIT project performance?

491. What deliverables come first?

492. What is it ?

493. Have the lessons learned been filed with the CGEIT project Management Office?

494. Vac -variance at completion, how much over/ under budget do you expect to be?

495. Has the CGEIT project (or CGEIT project phase)

been evaluated against each objective established in the product description and Integrated CGEIT project Plan?

496. Are you asking management for something as a result of this update?

497. What strengths do you have?

498. Is there anything unique in this CGEIT projects scope statement that will affect resources?

499. Impact to environment?

500. What is cost and CGEIT project cost management?

501. How concrete were original objectives?

2.24 Quality Management Plan: CGEIT

502. Who needs a qmp?

503. Is staff trained on the software technologies that are being used on the CGEIT project?

504. How does your organization design processes to ensure others meet customer and others requirements?

505. Are there nonconformance issues?

506. How does your organization recruit, hire, and retain new employees?

507. What has the QM Collaboration done?

508. Is there a Quality Management Plan?

509. How does your organization establish and maintain customer relationships?

510. What are your organizations key processes (product, service, business, and support)?

511. What is the audience for the data?

512. Are there processes in place to ensure internal consistency between the source code components?

513. What does it do for you (or to me)?

514. How does your organization use comparative

data and information to improve organizational performance?

515. Would impacts defined serve as impediments?

516. How does your organization perform analyzes to assess overall organizational performance and set priorities?

517. Contradictory information between different documents?

518. Where do you focus?

519. Was trending evident between reviews?

520. Show/provide copy of procedures for taking field notes?

2.25 Quality Metrics: CGEIT

521. How do you measure?

522. What are you trying to accomplish?

523. How can the effectiveness of each of the activities be measured?

524. Is there alignment within your organization on definitions?

525. Which are the right metrics to use?

526. What does this tell us?

527. Did the team meet the CGEIT project success criteria documented in the Quality Metrics Matrix?

528. Where did complaints, returns and warranty claims come from?

529. Which data do others need in one place to target areas of improvement?

530. Have alternatives been defined in the event that failure occurs?

531. Are quality metrics defined?

532. Have risk areas been identified?

533. Product Availability ?

534. Are there any open risk issues?

535. Are applicable standards referenced and available?

536. What is the timeline to meet your goal?

537. What about still open problems?

538. Can you correlate your quality metrics to profitability?

539. Can visual measures help you to filter visualizations of interest?

540. There are many reasons to shore up quality-related metrics, and what metrics are important?

2.26 Process Improvement Plan: CGEIT

541. What personnel are the change agents for your initiative?

542. What personnel are the coaches for your initiative?

543. Everyone agrees on what process improvement is, right?

544. What is the return on investment?

545. Purpose of goal: the motive is determined by asking, why do you want to achieve this goal?

546. To elicit goal statements, do you ask a question such as, What do you want to achieve?

547. What personnel are the champions for the initiative?

548. Are you making progress on the improvement framework?

549. Modeling current processes is great, and will you ever see a return on that investment?

550. Who should prepare the process improvement action plan?

551. Have the supporting tools been developed or

acquired?

552. How do you manage quality?

553. What lessons have you learned so far?

554. Has the time line required to move measurement results from the points of collection to databases or users been established?

555. Why quality management?

556. Does your process ensure quality?

557. What makes people good SPI coaches?

558. What actions are needed to address the problems and achieve the goals?

559. What is quality and how will you ensure it?

2.27 Responsibility Assignment Matrix: CGEIT

560. Are your organizations and items of cost assigned to each pool identified?

561. What is the primary purpose of the human resource plan?

562. Are all authorized tasks assigned to identified organizational elements?

563. What do you do when people do not respond?

564. Is cost and schedule performance measurement done in a consistent, systematic manner?

565. Competencies and craftsmanship – what competencies are necessary and what level?

566. When performing is split among two or more roles, is the work clearly defined so that the efforts are coordinated and the communication is clear?

567. Identify and isolate causes of favorable and unfavorable cost and schedule variances?

568. Ideas for developing soft skills at your organization?

569. Does the accounting system provide a basis for auditing records of direct costs chargeable to the contract?

570. Are the requirements for all items of overhead established by rational, traceable processes?

571. Can the contractor substantiate work package and planning package budgets?

572. Cwbs elements to be subcontracted, with identification of subcontractors?

573. Does the contractor use objective results, design reviews, and tests to trace schedule?

574. What expertise is not available in your department?

575. What cost control tool do many experts say is crucial to CGEIT project management?

576. With too many people labeled as doing the work, are there too many hands involved?

577. Are all elements of indirect expense identified to overhead cost budgets of CGEIT projections?

578. Do work packages consist of discrete tasks which are adequately described?

2.28 Roles and Responsibilities: CGEIT

579. Implementation of actions: Who are the responsible units?

580. Once the responsibilities are defined for the CGEIT project, have the deliverables, roles and responsibilities been clearly communicated to every participant?

581. What specific behaviors did you observe?

582. How is your work-life balance?

583. Who is involved?

584. Who is responsible for implementation activities and where will the functions, roles and responsibilities be defined?

585. Are CGEIT project team roles and responsibilities identified and documented?

586. What should you do now to prepare yourself for a promotion, increased responsibilities or a different job?

587. What should you highlight for improvement?

588. Is there a training program in place for stakeholders covering expectations, roles and responsibilities and any addition knowledge others need to be good stakeholders?

589. Are your policies supportive of a culture of quality data?

590. To decide whether to use a quality measurement, ask how will you know when it is achieved?

591. Have you ever been a part of this team?

592. Are governance roles and responsibilities documented?

593. What areas of supervision are challenging for you?

594. Where are you most strong as a supervisor?

595. How well did the CGEIT project Team understand the expectations of specific roles and responsibilities?

596. Authority: what areas/CGEIT projects in your work do you have the authority to decide upon and act on the already stated decisions?

597. Does the team have access to and ability to use data analysis tools?

2.29 Human Resource Management Plan: CGEIT

598. Does a documented CGEIT project organizational policy & plan (i.e. governance model) exist?

599. Have adequate resources been provided by management to ensure CGEIT project success?

600. Are the results of quality assurance reviews provided to affected groups & individuals?

601. What were things that you did very well and want to do the same again on the next CGEIT project?

602. Are the right people being attracted and retained to meet the future challenges?

603. Is the CGEIT project schedule available for all CGEIT project team members to review?

604. Are multiple estimation methods being employed?

605. Do people have the competencies to meet the strategic objectives?

606. List the assumptions made to date. What did you have to assume to be true to complete the charter?

607. Have activity relationships and interdependencies within tasks been adequately identified?

608. Measurable - are the targets measurable?

609. Have all team members been part of identifying risks?

610. Is there a formal set of procedures supporting Stakeholder Management?

611. Are issues raised, assessed, actioned, and resolved in a timely and efficient manner?

612. Were CGEIT project team members involved in the development of activity & task decomposition?

2.30 Communications Management Plan: CGEIT

613. Which stakeholders are thought leaders, influences, or early adopters?

614. Will messages be directly related to the release strategy or phases of the CGEIT project?

615. How did the term stakeholder originate?

616. Who is the stakeholder?

617. How much time does it take to do it?

618. What to know?

619. What communications method?

620. How were corresponding initiatives successful?

621. Can you think of other people who might have concerns or interests?

622. Are stakeholders internal or external?

623. Are there too many who have an interest in some aspect of your work?

624. Who will use or be affected by the result of a CGEIT project?

625. What steps can you take for a positive

relationship?

626. What is the political influence?

627. How do you manage communications?

628. Which team member will work with each stakeholder?

629. Are the stakeholders getting the information others need, are others consulted, are concerns addressed?

630. Is there an important stakeholder who is actively opposed and will not receive messages?

631. What to learn?

632. Where do team members get information?

2.31 Risk Management Plan: CGEIT

633. What would you do differently?

634. Do requirements demand the use of new analysis, design, or testing methods?

635. What is the likelihood?

636. Why might it be late?

637. What should be done with non-critical risks?

638. Is there anything you would now do differently on your CGEIT project based on this experience?

639. What risks are tracked?

640. Have you worked with the customer in the past?

641. Was an original risk assessment/risk management plan completed?

642. How are risk analvsis and prioritization performed?

643. What does a risk management program do?

644. Maximize short-term return on investment?

645. Risks should be identified during which phase of CGEIT project management life cycle?

646. Is the process supported by tools?

647. Can the risk be avoided by choosing a different alternative?

648. What is the likelihood that your organization would accept responsibility for the risk?

649. Why do you want risk management?

650. Have staff received necessary training?

651. Do requirements put excessive performance constraints on the product?

652. What will drive change?

2.32 Risk Register: CGEIT

653. User involvement: do you have the right users?

654. Are corrective measures implemented as planned?

655. What are the main aims, objectives of the policy, strategy, or service and the intended outcomes?

656. Are your objectives at risk?

657. What further options might be available for responding to the risk?

658. What could prevent you delivering on the strategic program objectives and what is being done to mitigate corresponding issues?

659. What would the impact to the CGEIT project objectives be should the risk arise?

660. What should you do when?

661. How well are risks controlled?

662. Manageability – have mitigations to the risk been identified?

663. Are implemented controls working as others should?

664. What are your key risks/show istoppers and what is being done to manage them?

665. Financial risk -can your organization afford to undertake the CGEIT project?

666. Is further information required before making a decision?

667. What is the reason for current performance gaps and do the risks and opportunities identified previously account for this?

668. Can the likelihood and impact of failing to achieve corresponding recommendations and action plans be assessed?

669. What is the appropriate level of risk management for this CGEIT project?

670. When would you develop a risk register?

671. How are risks identified?

672. What is a Risk?

2.33 Probability and Impact Assessment: CGEIT

673. Can this technology be absorbed with current level of expertise available in your organization?

674. Will new information become available during the CGEIT project?

675. Are tools for analysis and design available?

676. Are people attending meetings and doing work?

677. How completely has the customer been identified?

678. Would avoiding any of corresponding impact the CGEIT projects chance of success?

679. How do the products attain the specifications?

680. Are trained personnel, including supervisors and CGEIT project managers, available to handle such a large CGEIT project?

681. How is the CGEIT project going to be managed?

682. What is the risk appetite?

683. Are the best people available?

684. Anticipated volatility of the requirements?

685. Supply/demand CGEIT projections and trends; what are the levels of accuracy?

686. Do you use diagramming techniques to show cause and effect?

687. How carefully have the potential competitors been identified?

688. What would be the effect of slippage?

689. How do you maximize short-term return on investment?

690. Does the customer have a solid idea of what is required?

691. Which role do you have in the CGEIT project?

692. How solid is the CGEIT projection of competitive reaction?

2.34 Probability and Impact Matrix: CGEIT

693. How do risks change during the CGEIT projects life cycle?

694. Is the number of people on the CGEIT project team adequate to do the job?

695. What are data sources?

696. What can you use the analyzed risks for?

697. Is security a central objective?

698. Risk categorization -which of your categories has more risk than others?

699. How will the consumption pattern change?

700. Should the risk be taken at all?

701. Several experts are offsite, and wish to be included. How can this be done?

702. Who are the owners?

703. What are the levels of understanding of the future users of this technology?

704. How should you structure risks?

705. If you can not fix it, how do you do it differently?

706. How much is the probability of the risk occurring?

707. What is the level of commitment and professionalism?

708. What are the preparations required for facing difficulties?

709. Is a software CGEIT project management tool available?

2.35 Risk Data Sheet: CGEIT

710. What do you know?

711. What is the likelihood of it happening?

712. What is the environment within which you operate (social trends, economic, community values, broad based participation, national directions etc.)?

713. How reliable is the data source?

714. What do people affected think about the need for, and practicality of preventive measures?

715. What are the main opportunities available to you that you should grab while you can?

716. What were the Causes that contributed?

717. Are new hazards created?

718. What are the main threats to your existence?

719. What are you weak at and therefore need to do better?

720. What can happen?

721. What is the duration of infection (the length of time the host is infected with the organizm) in a normal healthy human host?

722. Risk of what?

723. Whom do you serve (customers)?

724. What was measured?

725. What if client refuses?

726. During work activities could hazards exist?

727. What can you do?

728. What are you trying to achieve (Objectives)?

729. Do effective diagnostic tests exist?

2.36 Procurement Management Plan: CGEIT

730. Alignment to strategic goals & objectives?

731. Are changes in deliverable commitments agreed to by all affected groups & individuals?

732. Is there a formal set of procedures supporting Issues Management?

733. How will multiple providers be managed?

734. Public engagement – did you get it right?

735. What are things that you need to improve?

736. Does the CGEIT project have a Statement of Work?

737. Is the CGEIT project sponsor clearly communicating the business case or rationale for why this CGEIT project is needed?

738. Do CGEIT project managers participating in the CGEIT project know the CGEIT projects true status first hand?

739. Are procurement deliverables arriving on time and to specification?

740. Is there a Steering Committee in place?

741. Have the procedures for identifying budget variances been followed?

742. Similar CGEIT projects?

743. Have all documents been archived in a CGEIT project repository for each release?

744. Are enough systems & user personnel assigned to the CGEIT project?

745. Have CGEIT project team accountabilities & responsibilities been clearly defined?

746. Are CGEIT project leaders committed to this CGEIT project full time?

747. Are there checklists created to determine if all quality processes are followed?

748. Are status reports received per the CGEIT project Plan?

749. Are post milestone CGEIT project reviews (PMPR) conducted with your organization at least once a year?

2.37 Source Selection Criteria: CGEIT

750. What should a Draft Request for Proposal (DRFP) include?

751. Are types/quantities of material, facilities appropriate?

752. How do you ensure an integrated assessment of proposals?

753. What instructions should be provided regarding oral presentations?

754. How and when do you enter into CGEIT project Procurement Management?

755. If the costs are normalized, please account for how the normalization is conducted. Is a cost realism analysis used?

756. How long will it take for the purchase cost to be the same as the lease cost?

757. Are there any common areas of weaknesses or deficiencies in the proposals in the competitive range?

758. How do you consolidate reviews and analysis of evaluators?

759. Do you ensure you evaluate what you asked for, not what you want to see or expect to see?

760. What should be considered when developing evaluation standards?

761. How are clarifications and communications appropriately used?

762. What does an evaluation address and what does a sample resemble?

763. Is experience evaluated?

764. What evidence should be provided regarding proposal evaluations?

765. When is it appropriate to issue a Draft Request for Proposal (DRFP)?

766. Is this a cost contract?

767. How do you manage procurement?

768. Are there any specific considerations that precludes offers from being selected as the awardee?

769. Who is on the Source Selection Advisory Committee?

2.38 Stakeholder Management Plan: CGEIT

770. What training requirements are there based upon the required skills and resources?

771. Are corrective actions and variances reported?

772. How will the equipment be verified?

773. Has a quality assurance plan been developed for the CGEIT project?

774. Are CGEIT project leaders committed to this CGEIT project full time?

775. Do you know what your customers expectations are regarding this process?

776. What guidelines or procedures currently exist that must be adhered to (eg departmental accounting procedures)?

777. Are all key components of a Quality Assurance Plan present?

778. Is the amount of effort justified by the anticipated value of forming a new process?

779. Have you eliminated all duplicative tasks or manual efforts, where appropriate?

780. Where does the information come from?

781. Describe the process that will be used to design, develop, review, accept, distribute and change outputs. Will all outputs delivered by the CGEIT project follow the same process?

782. Where are the verification requirements to be documented (eg purchase order, agreement etc)?

783. Are communication systems currently in place appropriate?

784. Is there an issues management plan in place?

785. What is meant by activity dependencies and how do they relate to network diagramming?

786. Are you meeting your customers expectations consistently?

787. Are risk oriented checklists used during risk identification?

2.39 Change Management Plan: CGEIT

788. Readiness -what is a successful end state?

789. Do there need to be new channels developed?

790. What processes are in place to manage knowledge about the CGEIT project?

791. What risks may occur upfront?

792. What does a resilient organization look like?

793. Who is the audience for change management activities?

794. Where do you want to be?

795. What are the dependencies?

796. What can you do to minimise misinterpretation and negative perceptions?

797. Why is the initiative is being undertaken - What are the business drivers?

798. Has the training provider been established?

799. What is the most cynical response it can receive?

800. How can you best frame the message so that it addresses the audiences interests?

801. Have the approved procedures and policies been

published?

802. How will the stakeholders share information and transfer knowledge?

803. What new roles are needed?

804. What method and medium would you use to announce a message?

805. Has the relevant business unit been notified of installation and support requirements?

806. Who is the target audience of the piece of information?

807. What are the current methods of sharing information and do there need to be new ones developed?

3.0 Executing Process Group: CGEIT

808. How does a CGEIT project life cycle differ from a product life cycle?

809. How is CGEIT project performance information created and distributed?

810. Who will provide training?

811. How can software assist in procuring goods and services?

812. What are the challenges CGEIT project teams face?

813. Do CGEIT project managers understand your organizational context for CGEIT projects?

814. Is activity definition the first process involved in CGEIT project time management?

815. How does CGEIT project management relate to other disciplines?

816. How can your organization use a weighted decision matrix to evaluate proposals as part of source selection?

817. What is the product of your CGEIT project?

818. What are deliverables of your CGEIT project?

819. What CGEIT projects and services are in the

portfolio of your organization?

820. How well did the chosen processes fit the needs of the CGEIT project?

821. Will a new application be developed using existing hardware, software, and networks?

822. Who are the CGEIT project stakeholders?

823. Will new hardware or software be required for servers or client machines?

824. Is the program supported by national and/or local organizations?

825. If a risk event occurs, what will you do?

3.1 Team Member Status Report: CGEIT

826. How does this product, good, or service meet the needs of the CGEIT project and your organization as a whole?

827. How it is to be done?

828. What specific interest groups do you have in place?

829. Why is it to be done?

830. How will resource planning be done?

831. When a teams productivity and success depend on collaboration and the efficient flow of information, what generally fails them?

832. How much risk is involved?

833. Is there evidence that staff is taking a more professional approach toward management of your organizations CGEIT projects?

834. Does every department have to have a CGEIT project Manager on staff?

835. Are the products of your organizations CGEIT projects meeting customers objectives?

836. What is to be done?

837. Are your organizations CGEIT projects more successful over time?

838. Do you have an Enterprise CGEIT project Management Office (EPMO)?

839. How can you make it practical?

840. Are the attitudes of staff regarding CGEIT project work improving?

841. The problem with Reward & Recognition Programs is that the truly deserving people all too often get left out. How can you make it practical?

842. Will the staff do training or is that done by a third party?

843. Does the product, good, or service already exist within your organization?

844. Does your organization have the means (staff, money, contract, etc.) to produce or to acquire the product, good, or service?

3.2 Change Request: CGEIT

845. Why were your requested changes rejected or not made?

846. When do you create a change request?

847. What are the duties of the change control team?

848. How well do experienced software developers predict software change?

849. Are change requests logged and managed?

850. How many times must the change be modified or presented to the change control board before it is approved?

851. Are there requirements attributes that are strongly related to the complexity and size?

852. Have all related configuration items been properly updated?

853. Why control change across the life cycle?

854. How can changes be graded?

855. What needs to be communicated?

856. What is the purpose of change control?

857. What is the change request log?

858. Should a more thorough impact analysis be conducted?

859. How to get changes (code) out in a timely manner?

860. Is it feasible to use requirements attributes as predictors of reliability?

861. Are there requirements attributes that can discriminate between high and low reliability?

862. Describe how modifications, enhancements, defects and/or deficiencies shall be notified (e.g. Problem Reports, Change Requests etc) and managed. Detail warranty and/or maintenance periods?

863. Will this change conflict with other requirements changes (e.g., lead to conflicting operational scenarios)?

864. Will all change requests and current status be logged?

3.3 Change Log: CGEIT

865. How does this change affect scope?

866. Does the suggested change request seem to represent a necessary enhancement to the product?

867. Is the change request open, closed or pending?

868. Is the change request within CGEIT project scope?

869. Does the suggested change request represent a desired enhancement to the products functionality?

870. Who initiated the change request?

871. When was the request approved?

872. Will the CGEIT project fail if the change request is not executed?

873. Is the change backward compatible without limitations?

874. How does this change affect the timeline of the schedule?

875. How does this relate to the standards developed for specific business processes?

876. Do the described changes impact on the integrity or security of the system?

877. When was the request submitted?

878. Where do changes come from?

879. Is the submitted change a new change or a modification of a previously approved change?

880. Is this a mandatory replacement?

881. Is the requested change request a result of changes in other CGEIT project(s)?

3.4 Decision Log: CGEIT

882. What is your overall strategy for quality control / quality assurance procedures?

883. How does an increasing emphasis on cost containment influence the strategies and tactics used?

884. What is the line where eDiscovery ends and document review begins?

885. What makes you different or better than others companies selling the same thing?

886. What are the cost implications?

887. What was the rationale for the decision?

888. Adversarial environment. is your opponent open to a non-traditional workflow, or will it likely challenge anything you do?

889. Do strategies and tactics aimed at less than full control reduce the costs of management or simply shift the cost burden?

890. Meeting purpose; why does this team meet?

891. It becomes critical to track and periodically revisit both operational effectiveness; Are you noticing all that you need to, and are you interpreting what you see effectively?

892. Is your opponent open to a non-traditional workflow, or will it likely challenge anything you do?

893. At what point in time does loss become unacceptable?

894. What alternatives/risks were considered?

895. How do you know when you are achieving it?

896. What is the average size of your matters in an applicable measurement?

897. Which variables make a critical difference?

898. Decision-making process; how will the team make decisions?

899. Who will be given a copy of this document and where will it be kept?

900. Behaviors; what are guidelines that the team has identified that will assist them with getting the most out of team meetings?

901. How effective is maintaining the log at facilitating organizational learning?

3.5 Quality Audit: CGEIT

902. How does your organization know that its information technology system is serving its needs as effectively and constructively as is appropriate?

903. What are the main things that hinder your ability to do a good job?

904. Are adequate and conveniently located toilet facilities available for use by the employees?

905. Are the intentions consistent with external obligations (such as applicable laws)?

906. How does your organization know that its Strategic Plan is providing the best guidance for the future of your organization?

907. How does your organization know that its support services planning and management systems are appropriately effective and constructive?

908. Quality is about improvement and accountability. The immediate questions that arise out of that statement are: (i) improvement on what, and (ii) accountable to whom?

909. Is the process of self review, learning and improvement endemic throughout your organization?

910. How does your organization know that it is maintaining a conducive staff climate?

911. What are you trying to accomplish with this audit?

912. What does the organizarion look for in a Quality audit?

913. How does your organization know that its system for inducting new staff to maximize workplace contributions are appropriately effective and constructive?

914. Are complaint files maintained?

915. How does your organization know that its range of activities are being reviewed as rigorously and constructively as they could be?

916. How does your organization know that its security arrangements are appropriately effective and constructive?

917. Is there a written corporate quality policy?

918. Is your organizational structure established and each positions responsibility defined?

919. How does the organization know that its system for maintaining and advancing the capabilities of its staff, particularly in relation to the Mission of the organization, is appropriately effective and constructive?

920. How does your organization know that its management of its ethical responsibilities is appropriately effective and constructive?

921. How does your organization know that its system for ensuring a positive organizational climate is appropriately effective and constructive?

3.6 Team Directory: CGEIT

922. Who will report CGEIT project status to all stakeholders?

923. Is construction on schedule?

924. Who will write the meeting minutes and distribute?

925. Process decisions: how well was task order work performed?

926. Process decisions: do job conditions warrant additional actions to collect job information and document on-site activity?

927. Who are the Team Members?

928. How will you accomplish and manage the objectives?

929. What are you going to deliver or accomplish?

930. Contract requirements complied with?

931. Who should receive information (all stakeholders)?

932. Process decisions: are contractors adequately prosecuting the work?

933. Where should the information be distributed?

934. When will you produce deliverables?

935. Why is the work necessary?

936. Process decisions: do invoice amounts match accepted work in place?

937. Process decisions: which organizational elements and which individuals will be assigned management functions?

938. How will the team handle changes?

3.7 Team Operating Agreement: CGEIT

939. Resource allocation: how will individual team members account for time and expenses, and how will this be allocated in the team budget?

940. Do you record meetings for the already stated unable to attend?

941. Must your team members rely on the expertise of other members to complete tasks?

942. What administrative supports will be put in place to support the team and the teams supervisor?

943. Must your members collaborate successfully to complete CGEIT projects?

944. Did you draft the meeting agenda?

945. Does your team need access to all documents and information at all times?

946. Seconds for members to respond?

947. What is your unique contribution to your organization?

948. Are there more than two functional areas represented by your team?

949. Do you post any action items, due dates, and

responsibilities on the team website?

950. Conflict resolution: how will disputes and other conflicts be mediated or resolved?

951. What resources can be provided for the team in terms of equipment, space, time for training, protected time and space for meetings, and travel allowances?

952. To whom do you deliver your services?

953. What is a Virtual Team?

954. Confidentiality: how will confidential information be handled?

955. Do team members reside in more than two countries?

956. How will you resolve conflict efficiently and respectfully?

957. Communication protocols: how will the team communicate?

958. Did you determine the technology methods that best match the messages to be communicated?

3.8 Team Performance Assessment: CGEIT

959. To what degree can team members meet frequently enough to accomplish the teams ends?

960. How do you keep key people outside the group informed about its accomplishments?

961. To what degree are the members clear on what they are individually responsible for and what they are jointly responsible for?

962. Does more radicalness mean more perceived benefits?

963. Lack of method variance in self-reported affect and perceptions at work: Reality or artifact?

964. To what degree do team members feel that the purpose of the team is important, if not exciting?

965. How does CGEIT project termination impact CGEIT project team members?

966. To what degree do all members feel responsible for all agreed-upon measures?

967. How do you encourage members to learn from each other?

968. To what degree does the teams approach to its work allow for modification and improvement over

time?

969. What are you doing specifically to develop the leaders around you?

970. To what degree are the relative importance and priority of the goals clear to all team members?

971. To what degree is the team cognizant of small wins to be celebrated along the way?

972. When a reviewer complains about method variance, what is the essence of the complaint?

973. Can familiarity breed backup?

974. To what degree does the teams purpose constitute a broader, deeper aspiration than just accomplishing short-term goals?

975. To what degree will team members, individually and collectively, commit time to help themselves and others learn and develop skills?

976. How much interpersonal friction is there in your team?

977. What are teams?

978. To what degree do team members frequently explore the teams purpose and its implications?

3.9 Team Member Performance Assessment: CGEIT

979. Who is responsible?

980. To what degree will new and supplemental skills be introduced as the need is recognized?

981. Is it critical or vital to the job?

982. What variables that affect team members achievement are within your control?

983. How are assessments designed, delivered, and otherwise used to maximize training?

984. How will you identify your Team Leaders?

985. What were the challenges that resulted for training and assessment?

986. What happens if a team member disagrees with the Job Expectations?

987. How is your organizations Strategic Management System tied to performance measurement?

988. In what areas would you like to concentrate your knowledge and resources?

989. Who should attend?

990. What are the standards or expectations for

success?

991. What are they responsible for?

992. What is collaboration?

993. To what extent did the evaluation influence the instructional path, such as with adaptive testing?

994. To what degree is there a sense that only the team can succeed?

995. To what degree can team members frequently and easily communicate with one another?

3.10 Issue Log: CGEIT

996. What does the stakeholder need from the team?

997. Are the stakeholders getting the information they need, are they consulted, are concerns addressed?

998. What is the status of the issue?

999. What approaches do you use?

1000. Is the issue log kept in a safe place?

1001. What effort will a change need?

1002. Why not more evaluators?

1003. Persistence; will users learn a work around or will they be bothered every time?

1004. Who are the members of the governing body?

1005. Are the CGEIT project issues uniquely identified, including to which product they refer?

1006. Are stakeholder roles recognized by your organization?

1007. What are the stakeholders interrelationships?

1008. What would have to change?

1009. What steps can you take for positive

relationships?

1010. Who were proponents/opponents?

1011. Who is the issue assigned to?

1012. Are you constantly rushing from meeting to meeting?

4.0 Monitoring and Controlling Process Group: CGEIT

1013. What kinds of things in particular are you looking for data on?

1014. How should needs be met?

1015. How are you doing?

1016. How will staff learn how to use the deliverables?

1017. Is there undesirable impact on staff or resources?

1018. Is the program making progress in helping to achieve the set results?

1019. Who are the CGEIT project stakeholders?

1020. What is the timeline for the CGEIT project?

1021. Accuracy: what design will lead to accurate information?

1022. Contingency planning. if a risk event occurs, what will you do?

1023. Is it what was agreed upon?

1024. What departments are involved in its daily operation?

1025. What resources (both financial and non-financial) are available/needed?

1026. What is the expected monetary value of the CGEIT project?

1027. How many potential communications channels exist on the CGEIT project?

1028. How well did the chosen processes fit the needs of the CGEIT project?

1029. How to ensure validity, quality and consistency?

4.1 Project Performance Report: CGEIT

1030. To what degree does the informal organization make use of individual resources and meet individual needs?

1031. To what degree can the cognitive capacity of individuals accommodate the flow of information?

1032. To what degree do team members articulate the teams work approach?

1033. To what degree are fresh input and perspectives systematically caught and added (for example, through information and analysis, new members, and senior sponsors)?

1034. How can CGEIT project sustainability be maintained?

1035. How will procurement be coordinated with other CGEIT project aspects, such as scheduling and performance reporting?

1036. To what degree are the demands of the task compatible with and converge with the relationships of the informal organization?

1037. To what degree are sub-teams possible or necessary?

1038. To what degree does the teams purpose

contain themes that are particularly meaningful and memorable?

1039. To what degree are the tasks requirements reflected in the flow and storage of information?

1040. To what degree does the task meet individual needs?

1041. To what degree are the skill areas critical to team performance present?

1042. To what degree will the team ensure that all members equitably share the work essential to the success of the team?

1043. To what degree is there centralized control of information sharing?

1044. To what degree do the relationships of the informal organization motivate taskrelevant behavior and facilitate task completion?

1045. To what degree can the team measure progress against specific goals?

4.2 Variance Analysis: CGEIT

1046. Historical experience?

1047. Contract line items and end items?

1048. Are detailed work packages planned as far in advance as practicable?

1049. Budget versus actual. how does the monthly budget compare to actual experience?

1050. Are indirect costs charged to the appropriate indirect pools and incurring organization?

1051. How are variances affected by multiple material and labor categories?

1052. Are indirect costs accumulated for comparison with the corresponding budgets?

1053. Is there a logical explanation for any variance?

1054. Are all budgets assigned to control accounts?

1055. How have the setting and use of standards changed over time?

1056. What is the incurrence of actual indirect costs in excess of budgets, by element of expense?

1057. How do you haverify authorization to proceed with all authorized work?

1058. Did your organization lose existing customers and/or gain new customers?

1059. What business event causes fluctuations?

1060. Do the rates and prices remain constant throughout the year?

1061. Are material costs reported within the same period as that in which BCWP is earned for that material?

1062. How do you identify potential or actual overruns and underruns?

4.3 Earned Value Status: CGEIT

1063. When is it going to finish?

1064. How does this compare with other CGEIT projects?

1065. Earned value can be used in almost any CGEIT project situation and in almost any CGEIT project environment. it may be used on large CGEIT projects, medium sized CGEIT projects, tiny CGEIT projects (in cut-down form), complex and simple CGEIT projects and in any market sector. some people, of course, know all about earned value, they have used it for years - but perhaps not as effectively as they could have?

1066. Validation is a process of ensuring that the developed system will actually achieve the stakeholders desired outcomes; Are you building the right product? What do you validate?

1067. Verification is a process of ensuring that the developed system satisfies the stakeholders agreements and specifications; Are you building the product right? What do you haverify?

1068. Where is evidence-based earned value in your organization reported?

1069. What is the unit of forecast value?

1070. Are you hitting your CGEIT projects targets?

1071. If earned value management (EVM) is so good in determining the true status of a CGEIT project and CGEIT project its completion, why is it that hardly any one uses it in information systems related CGEIT projects?

1072. How much is it going to cost by the finish?

1073. Where are your problem areas?

4.4 Risk Audit: CGEIT

1074. Is the customer willing to establish rapid communication links with the developer?

1075. Do you record and file all audits?

1076. How are risk appetites expressed?

1077. To what extent should analytical procedures be utilized in the risk-assessment process?

1078. Are you meeting your legal, regulatory and compliance requirements - if not, why not?

1079. Are corresponding safety and risk management policies posted for all to see?

1080. Are auditors able to effectively apply more soft evidence found in the risk-assessment process with the results of more tangible audit evidence found through more substantive testing?

1081. Are CGEIT project requirements stable?

1082. What events or circumstances could affect the achievement of your objectives?

1083. Assessing risk with analytical procedures: do systemsthinking tools help auditors focus on diagnostic patterns?

1084. Is the customer technically sophisticated in the product area?

1085. What are risks and how do you manage them?

1086. What risk does not having unique identification present?

1087. Is your organization willing to commit significant time to the requirements gathering process?

1088. Are testing tools available and suitable?

1089. Is a software CGEIT project management tool available?

1090. Does your organization have a register of insurance policies detailing all current insurance policies?

1091. Are risk management strategies documented?

1092. How effective are your risk controls?

1093. Are enough people available?

4.5 Contractor Status Report: CGEIT

1094. What are the minimum and optimal bandwidth requirements for the proposed soluiton?

1095. If applicable; describe your standard schedule for new software version releases. Are new software version releases included in the standard maintenance plan?

1096. What was the final actual cost?

1097. Are there contractual transfer concerns?

1098. What process manages the contracts?

1099. How long have you been using the services?

1100. What was the budget or estimated cost for your organizations services?

1101. Who can list a CGEIT project as organization experience, your organization or a previous employee of your organization?

1102. What is the average response time for answering a support call?

1103. How is risk transferred?

1104. What was the actual budget or estimated cost for your organizations services?

1105. How does the proposed individual meet each

requirement?

1106. What was the overall budget or estimated cost?

1107. Describe how often regular updates are made to the proposed solution. Are corresponding regular updates included in the standard maintenance plan?

4.6 Formal Acceptance: CGEIT

1108. What is the Acceptance Management Process?

1109. Was business value realized?

1110. Is formal acceptance of the CGEIT project product documented and distributed?

1111. Does it do what client said it would?

1112. Did the CGEIT project achieve its MOV?

1113. What was done right?

1114. Was the client satisfied with the CGEIT project results?

1115. Was the CGEIT project work done on time, within budget, and according to specification?

1116. How does your team plan to obtain formal acceptance on your CGEIT project?

1117. Was the CGEIT project goal achieved?

1118. Who would use it?

1119. Does it do what CGEIT project team said it would?

1120. What lessons were learned about your CGEIT project management methodology?

1121. General estimate of the costs and times to complete the CGEIT project?

1122. Was the CGEIT project managed well?

1123. Do you perform formal acceptance or burn-in tests?

1124. Have all comments been addressed?

1125. Was the sponsor/customer satisfied?

1126. How well did the team follow the methodology?

1127. Did the CGEIT project manager and team act in a professional and ethical manner?

5.0 Closing Process Group: CGEIT

1128. Did you do things well?

1129. What could be done to improve the process?

1130. What will you do to minimize the impact should a risk event occur?

1131. Were risks identified and mitigated?

1132. Does the close educate others to improve performance?

1133. How well did you do?

1134. What went well?

1135. What were things that you need to improve?

1136. Was the user/client satisfied with the end product?

1137. Is this a follow-on to a previous CGEIT project?

1138. What areas does the group agree are the biggest success on the CGEIT project?

1139. Did you do what you said you were going to do?

1140. Were cost budgets met?

1141. What is the amount of funding and what CGEIT project phases are funded?

1142. What is the CGEIT project Management Process?

1143. Can the lesson learned be replicated?

1144. How will you do it?

1145. Mitigate. what will you do to minimize the impact should a risk event occur?

5.1 Procurement Audit: CGEIT

1146. Where applicable, did your organization adequately manage experts employed to assist in the procurement process?

1147. Are the supporting documents for payments voided or cancelled following payment?

1148. Are proper financing arrangements taken?

1149. Was your organization specific about the nature and scope of the performance before launching the procurement process?

1150. Are procedures established on how orders will be shipped?

1151. Are advantages and disadvantages of in-house production, outsourcing and Public Private Partnerships considered?

1152. Are individuals with check-signing responsibility prohibited from signing blank checks?

1153. Are idle funds invested, and is interest distributed to the various activity accounts at least annually?

1154. Are petty cash funds operated on an imprest basis?

1155. Was additional significant information supplied to all interested parties?

1156. Did the conditions included in the contract protect the risk of non-performance by the supplier and were there no conflicting provisions?

1157. Are signature plates under the control of someone other than the individual given check-signing accountability?

1158. Are all purchase orders reviewed by someone other than the individual preparing the purchase order (reasonableness of order and vendor selection)?

1159. When tenders were actually rejected because they were abnormally low, were reasons for this decision given and were they sufficiently grounded?

1160. Is it assessed whether well-functioning markets exist for the departments services/tasks?

1161. Are periodic audits made of disbursement activities?

1162. Was the chosen procedure the most efficient and effective for the performance of the contract?

1163. Are incentives to deliver on time and in quantity properly specified?

1164. Are procurement processes well organized and documented?

1165. Are there regular accounting reconciliations of contract payments, transactions and inventory?

5.2 Contract Close-Out: CGEIT

1166. Have all contracts been completed?

1167. Parties: who is involved?

1168. What is capture management?

1169. Have all acceptance criteria been met prior to final payment to contractors?

1170. What happens to the recipient of services?

1171. Was the contract sufficiently clear so as not to result in numerous disputes and misunderstandings?

1172. How/when used ?

1173. Change in attitude or behavior?

1174. Are the signers the authorized officials?

1175. Change in circumstances?

1176. Was the contract type appropriate?

1177. Have all contract records been included in the CGEIT project archives?

1178. Have all contracts been closed?

1179. Parties: Authorized?

1180. How is the contracting office notified of the

automatic contract close-out?

1181. Has each contract been audited to verify acceptance and delivery?

1182. Why Outsource?

1183. Change in knowledge?

1184. How does it work?

1185. Was the contract complete without requiring numerous changes and revisions?

5.3 Project or Phase Close-Out: CGEIT

1186. What process was planned for managing issues/ risks?

1187. Is the lesson significant, valid, and applicable?

1188. Were the outcomes different from the already stated planned?

1189. What can you do better next time, and what specific actions can you take to improve?

1190. What benefits or impacts does the stakeholder group expect to obtain as a result of the CGEIT project?

1191. What stakeholder group needs, expectations, and interests are being met by the CGEIT project?

1192. Planned remaining costs?

1193. What is a Risk Management Process?

1194. What was expected from each stakeholder?

1195. Who are the CGEIT project stakeholders and what are roles and involvement?

1196. What are the mandatory communication needs for each stakeholder?

1197. Which changes might a stakeholder be required to make as a result of the CGEIT project?

1198. What was the preferred delivery mechanism?

1199. Complete yes or no?

1200. What is in it for you?

1201. What information did each stakeholder need to contribute to the CGEIT projects success?

1202. If you were the CGEIT project sponsor, how would you determine which CGEIT project team(s) and/or individuals deserve recognition?

1203. What are the informational communication needs for each stakeholder?

5.4 Lessons Learned: CGEIT

1204. How well do you feel the executives supported this CGEIT project?

1205. What worked well or did not work well, either for this CGEIT project or for the CGEIT project team?

1206. What on the CGEIT project worked well and was effective in the delivery of the product?

1207. How timely were Progress Reports provided to the CGEIT project Manager by Team Members?

1208. Overall, how effective were the efforts to prepare you and your organization for the impact of the product/service of the CGEIT project?

1209. Was the change control process properly implemented to manage changes to cost, scope, schedule, or quality?

1210. How adequately involved did you feel in CGEIT project decisions?

1211. How well did the scope of the CGEIT project match what was defined in the CGEIT project Proposal?

1212. Were the CGEIT project goals attained?

1213. What were the most significant issues on this CGEIT project?

1214. How well was CGEIT project status communicated throughout your involvement in the CGEIT project?

1215. How useful was your testing?

1216. What solutions or recommendations can you offer that would have improved some aspect of the CGEIT project?

1217. Did the CGEIT project change significantly?

1218. How useful was the format and content of the CGEIT project Status Report to you?

1219. Is there a clear cause and effect between the activity and the lesson learned?

1220. How effective was the support you received during implementation of the product/service?

1221. How much of your time was spent on other than this CGEIT project?

1222. How much flexibility is there in the funding (e.g., what authorities does the program manager have to change to the specifics of the funding within the overall funding ceiling)?

Index

countries   220
counts 105
course 29, 44, 233
covered   119
covering   9, 87, 180
covers 164
coworker   108
craziest   104
create 11, 23, 69, 100-101, 111, 138, 208
created   59, 81, 122, 126, 129, 194, 197, 204
creating   7, 51
creativity   75
credible   168
crisis   18
criteria 2, 5, 9, 11, 26, 32, 38, 72, 86, 91, 107, 117, 133, 136, 164,
168, 174, 198, 245
CRITERION   2, 17, 26, 39, 52, 63, 77, 88
critical 33, 37, 56, 59, 66, 76, 82, 85, 96, 115, 144-145, 152, 212-
213, 223, 230
criticism   59
cross-sell   89
crucial 57, 158, 179
crystal 13
cultural74
culture 27, 60, 126, 130, 181
current37, 39, 45, 50, 56, 60-62, 64, 72, 81, 90, 93, 99, 103-104,
153, 176, 189-190, 203, 209, 236
currently   32, 105, 200-201
custom23
customer   11, 24, 27-30, 33, 37, 75, 81, 84, 99, 109, 111, 115-
116, 172, 186, 190-191, 235, 240
customers   1, 19-20, 28-29, 32, 48, 50-51, 60-61, 89, 91, 93, 98,
102-104, 108, 115-116, 129, 138, 195, 200-201, 206, 232
cut-down   233
cynical202
damage   1
Dashboard   9
dashboards   78
database   158
databases   177
day-to-day   80, 105, 151
deadlines   23, 97, 123
dealing   19

multiple   132, 182, 196, 231
narrow 58
national   123, 125, 194, 205
nature 39, 243
nearest   13
nearly 106
necessary   48, 60, 67, 91, 96, 111, 129, 169, 178, 187, 210, 218, 229
needed   18-19, 22-23, 36, 53, 80-81, 86, 160, 164, 166, 177, 196, 203, 228
negative   112, 202
negotiate   108
negotiated   99
neither 1
network   3, 153-154, 201
networks   158, 205
Neutral 12, 17, 26, 39, 52, 63, 77, 88
normal 82, 194
normalized   198
Notice 1
noticing   212
notified   203, 209, 245
number   25, 38, 43, 51, 62, 76, 87, 116, 150, 192, 251
numbers   110, 159
numerous   245-246
objective   7, 48, 118, 143, 171, 179, 192
objectives   19, 22, 24, 26-27, 34, 51, 53, 61, 84, 86, 95, 106-107, 112, 115, 123, 162, 170-171, 182, 188, 195-196, 206, 217, 235
observe   180
observed   66
observing   140
obsolete   107
obstacles   21, 151, 161, 169
obtain 103, 239, 247
obtained   33, 49, 129
obvious   112
obviously   12
occurring   73, 193
occurs 18, 81, 174, 205, 227
offerings   61, 68
offers   199
office   138, 164, 170, 207, 245
officials 245

276

purpose   2, 11, 110, 120, 156, 162, 169-170, 176, 178, 208, 212, 221-222, 229
pushing   104
qualified   29, 128, 138, 145
qualities   22
quality 1, 4-5, 11, 40, 44, 47, 57, 62, 81, 85, 114, 124, 129-130, 137-138, 145, 158, 167, 172, 174-175, 177, 181-182, 197, 200, 212, 214-215, 228, 249
quantities   198
quantity   244
question   12-13, 17, 26, 39, 52, 63, 77, 88, 102, 176
questions   7, 9, 12, 53, 138, 158, 214
quickly 11, 53, 55, 57, 59
radically   55
raised 137, 183
rather 39, 91
rating 164
rational   179
rationale   196, 212
reached   22
reaching   95
reaction   191
reactivate   104
Readiness   202
readings   85
realism 198
realistic   22, 106
Reality 221
realized   109, 239
really   7, 33, 102, 131
reason 99, 116, 189
reasonable   93, 146
reasonably   143
reasons   37, 175, 244
re-assign   149
rebuild 111
receive   9-10, 34, 41, 185, 202, 217
received   35, 103, 145, 187, 197, 250
recently   11, 99
recipient   21, 245
recognised   69
recognize   2, 17-20, 43, 67, 73
recognized   18-23, 57, 223, 225

284

result   55, 69, 71, 137, 166, 168, 171, 184, 211, 245, 247
resulted   78, 223
resulting   60, 127
results 9, 31, 33, 43, 61, 63, 67-70, 75, 83-84, 125, 127, 150, 169,
177, 179, 182, 227, 235, 239
retain 88, 172
retained   182
retrospect   89
return 43, 69, 111, 176, 186, 191
returns 174
revenue   24, 51
review 11, 42, 154, 182, 201, 212, 214
reviewed   29, 137, 145-146, 162, 164, 215, 244
reviewer   222
reviews11, 139, 154, 173, 179, 182, 197-198
revised 61, 78
revisions   246
revisit 212
reward 46, 51, 57, 207
rewarded   20
rewards   78
rework 44
rights   1
rigorously   215
robustness   124
routine 81, 144
rushing 226
safeguard   124
safeguards   102
safety 98, 235
sample199
sampling   130
satisfied   93, 131, 166, 239-241
satisfies233
satisfying   115
savings33, 61
scenarios   209
schedule   3-4, 32, 42, 73, 81, 94, 131, 143, 145-146, 153-154,
159, 162-164, 178-179, 182, 210, 217, 237, 249
scheduled   166
schedules   143, 162-163
scheduling   229
scheme   78

short-term   186, 191, 222
should 7, 23, 31, 35, 38, 41, 57, 64-66, 68, 70, 80, 82, 92-93, 95-97, 100, 103, 118, 122, 125, 127, 131, 139, 147, 149, 151, 156, 162, 166-167, 176, 180, 186, 188, 192, 194, 198-199, 209, 217, 223, 227, 235, 241-242
signature   101, 244
signatures   155
signers 245
signing 243
similar 30-31, 55, 61, 68, 149-150, 165, 197
simple 95, 233
simply 9, 11, 212
single   102
single-use   7
situation   25, 39, 118, 233
situations   81
skeptical   94
skills   18, 22, 48, 97-98, 102, 159, 178, 200, 222-223
slippage   191
smallest   17, 69
social 94, 194
societal   111
software   18, 131, 158, 162, 172, 193, 204-205, 208, 236-237
solicit 28
soluiton   237
solution   45, 53, 60, 63, 65, 67, 71-74, 77, 139, 238
solutions   50, 64-65, 68, 72, 74, 250
someone   7, 244
something   106, 127, 171
Sometimes   50
source 5, 96, 113, 172, 194, 198-199, 204
sources   28, 55, 61, 74, 192
special 84
specific   9, 18, 27, 29, 32, 58, 70, 97, 118, 147, 152-153, 155-156, 180-181, 199, 206, 210, 230, 243, 247
specifics   250
specified   95, 143, 244
Speech   133
spoken 99
sponsor   24, 127, 196, 240, 248
sponsored   30
sponsors   19, 166, 229
stability 48, 137

CPSIA information can be obtained
at www.ICGtesting.com
Printed in the USA
BVHW081233120819
555664BV00024B/2386/P